Praise for *A New Way to Be Human*

"If you are searching to create a holistic spiritual framework of love, compassion, justice, and mercy, this book will become a wondrous companion. It is a glorious invitation to the spiritual quest."
—Nora Gallagher, author of *Practicing Resurrection* and *Things Seen and Unseen: A Year Lived in Faith*

"Reading [Robert's] story, and particularly the life challenges he was able to overcome, you will become inspired to move beyond your own difficulties into a life of deeper purpose."
—Jonathan Klein, CEO of Getty Images

"*A New Way to Be Human* could not be a more timely guide. Every day, I hear from people who are looking for more peace and wholeness in their lives, and now I know just what to hand them. For anyone craving authenticity, but may not know exactly what the 'real them' looks like... this is exactly the book you need. I chuckled and got choked up reading Robert's colorful and inspiring life stories."
—Elizabeth Wiatt, environmentalist, philanthropist, and co-founder of Fashionology

"At a time when many struggle to find authentic meaning in their lives, Robert Taylor has given us a guide. Well written, humble, and powerful, *A New Way to Be Human* is a roadmap for a life well-lived. Everyone who has ever wondered 'why am I here?' should read this book."
—Trevor Neilson, president, Global Philanthropy Group

"No matter who you are or what you believe this book will change your life—discover how transforming it is to see the world through eyes of love, a heart of compassion, a mind of wisdom, and a spirit of wonder!"
—Rabbi Irwin Kula, author of *Yearnings: Embracing the Sacred Messiness of Life*

"*A New Way to Be Human* is a majestic, powerful work. Grounded in the rich legacy of Ubuntu, Robert invites us into a wondrous landscape, a realm governed by gratitude, compassion, and mercy, a world where grace reigns."
—Dr. Gloria J. Burgess, author of *Legacy Living* and *Dare to Wear Your Soul on the Outside: Live Your Legacy NOW*

"This is the ideal book for someone like me and many others I know—those who don't consider themselves religious, but aspire to want to live meaningful, compassionate, and impactful lives. Robert gives us a framework for leading that kind of life—one that is true to my nature. His is among the first books that doesn't just make me admire the author, but makes ME want to be bolder."
—Mitchell Gold, co-founder of Mitchell Gold + Bob Williams Furniture Design, and founder of Faith in America

"In Robert's redemption and liberation we hear a call to redeem and liberate the whole human family. Soak it in. Then live it out."
—Robin R. Meyers, author of *The Underground Church*

"This is a book that I'm going to keep on that special shelf in my study where I turn for inspiration when I need encouragement, hope when I'm despairing, and courage when I'm feeling scared. Robert's wisdom challenges us to face the obstacles and possibilities of our lives with courage, conviction, and humor: I am without a doubt recommending this book to fellow seekers who come my way."
—The Very Rev. Tracey Lind, Dean of Trinity Cathedral, Cleveland, Ohio

"I have never read a book quite like it. This book is a treasure. Robert V. Taylor has lived a life in which he was confronted with extremely stressful situations many times. Through it all he was forced to find solutions to problems he never thought he would have to face. In the process he accumulated a vast understanding of the stretchablity of the human personality and its resilience in adjusting to difficult circumstances."
—Joseph F. Girzone, author of the Joshua series

"In a time when we are all searching for meaning in our life, *A New Way to Be Human* draws the reader in, expanding our thinking, opening our hearts, helping us discover our connection to one another. He shares his own personal struggles and weaves together many spiritual practices and traditions to help us enrich our own personal journey. Robert V. Taylor's underlying message is to treat ourselves and others with love and compassion. This is a book that I keep as a companion to my daily prayers and reflection."

—Paula Clapp, co-founder of Global Partnerships

"Taylor offers rich context, comfort, and guidance for those who want to move forward down the path of defining the role spirituality can play in leading an ethical life."

—Ric Merrifield, author of *rethink: A Business Manifesto for Cutting Costs and Boosting Innovation*

"Our great challenge in life is to be ourselves instead of perpetually trying to be someone else. Robert Taylor's book helps us meet this challenge head-on, with compassion and grace."

—Eric Elnes, author of *The Phoenix Affirmations*

"Perfect for our times! Robert's writings bring together the best lessons from the world's many faith traditions, applying them to modern life in a way that is profound and meaningful."

—Margaret Larson, documentary producer and Emmy Award journalist for *The Today Show* and *Dateline*

"If seminaries and other graduate schools ever get around to offering courses in imagination, this book needs to be required reading at every level. "

—Louie Crew, founder of Integrity USA and retired professor of English Literature, Rutgers University

"Religion invites exclusivity. Robert V. Taylor invites his readers to the inclusion message of love which unites us. He draws from his personal history and from a profound awareness of humanity's common quest for the Creator who resides in creation and in each of us."

—Paul J. Donoghue, SM, PhD, author of *Sick and Tired of Feeling Sick and Tired*

"A fascinating book that makes you see spirituality in a fresh and honest way. A wonderful book for getting life on track to lead a fulfilling life."

—Ginny Hutchinson, author of *Better Because of You*

"This book is like having your own spiritual director at the ready to lead you; one who is kind, empathetic, and experienced. Refreshingly, this guide is not "religious"...it is written for all who are interested in a spiritual path that fully embraces life."

—Chris Glaser, author of *The Final Deadline: What Death Has Taught Me About Life*

"This is spiritual magic, sweet as a ripe red strawberry."

—Andrew Himes, author of *The Sword of the Lord*

"Robert's writing is personal, potent, and provocative. He weaves together a roadmap to engage any searcher. Readers will emerge from the currents of his narrative with questions and ideas as well as a few—or many—answers that work for them."

—Judy Pigott, coauthor of *Personal Safety Nets*

"*A New Way to Be Human* is a bold and invigorating invitation to imagine a new path into our deepest, most spiritual core. Robert V. Taylor invites us to honor the "dignity of difference" within our common humanity.... The reader knows she is on a special encounter. Slowly reflect and savor the wisdom of this book."

—Dr. Judy Mayotte, Marquette University and author of *Disposable People? The Plight of Refugees*

"A worthy contribution to the emerging canon of spiritual self-awareness toward a common good."

—Rabbi Daniel A. Weiner, author of *Good God*

A New Way to Be Human

A New Way
to Be Human

7 Spiritual Pathways to Becoming Fully Alive

By Robert V. Taylor
Foreword by Desmond M. Tutu

A Division of The Career Press, Inc.
Pompton Plains, NJ

A NEW WAY TO BE HUMAN
EDITED BY KATHRYN HENCHES
TYPESET BY GINA TALUCCI
Cover design by Howard Grossman/12E Design
Printed in the U.S.A.

To order this title, please call toll-free 1-800-CAREER-1 (NJ and Canada: 201-848-0310) to order using VISA or MasterCard, or for further information on books from Career Press.

The Career Press, Inc.
220 West Parkway, Unit 12
Pompton Plains, NJ 07444
www.careerpress.com
www.newpagebooks.com

Library of Congress Cataloging-in-Publication Data
Taylor, Robert V., 1958-
        A new way to be human : 7 spiritual pathways to becoming fully alive /
by Robert V. Taylor ; foreword by Desmond M.
Tutu.
                p. cm.
        Includes index.
        ISBN 978-1-60163-215-9 -- ISBN 978-1-60163-600-3 (ebook) 1.
Spiritual life. 2. Self-actualization (Psychology)--Religious
aspects. 3. Conduct of life. I. Title.

BL624.T39 2012
204'.4--dc23

                                                              2012000062

This book is dedicated to those whose stories reveal the journey of a new way to be human, and to Jerry, who radiates love and joy.

Acknowledgments

Like the journey on a new way to being human, this book reflects a journey to becoming fully alive. I am filled with gratitude to all of those who have shaped, formed, challenged, and given me life and sustenance along the way. This book would not be possible without you. Our journeys are all interconnected on the path to becoming fully alive.

To the early readers of the manuscript for their truth-telling, support, and engagement, I am eternally grateful: Dorothy Papadakos, Eric Liu, Kathryn Hinsch, Louie Crew, Anne Kitch, Ryan Marriott, Leif Tellmann, Marlen Valencia, David "Sky Jubilee" Enroth, Paula Clapp, Wayne Burrows, Donna Blackwell, and Janice Condit, whose wise editorial suggestions were a blessing.

Paula Clapp is the spiritual mother of this book. Her rare friendship, encouragement, and belief in the message of this work has been a source of inspiration.

Archbishop Desmond Tutu is a constant friend whose loyalty, affection, and generosity I hope to offer in similar measure to others along the way.

My agent at Andrea Hurst Literary Agency, Gordon Warnock, has been a companion along the journey, never shy to offer advice with gentle wisdom and humor.

Judy Mikalonis is an extraordinary writing coach who has pushed me to greater clarity and focus while also being a passionate believer in the message of the book.

The team at New Page Books—Adam Schwartz, Michael Pye, and Laurie Kelly-Pye—is responsive and focused, and it is a profound pleasure to work with them.

Lucy, my Chocolate Labrador, has spent countless hours in my office as I have written, and unfailingly reminded me to be grounded by taking her out to fetch and play.

Jerry has been there at every step along this journey. In moments of doubt he is encouraging, supporting, and believing. In moments of new insight and transformation, he is there to celebrate. For such love, partnership, playfulness, delight, and abundant love, I give thanks.

To all who point the way to compassion, love, justice, hope, oneness, delight, and joy—this book is yours.

Contents

Foreword

The spiritual life is always an invitation to be authentically human in all of our grittiness, especially as we enter more deeply into the mystery of Love. It is in the crucible of life and Love that we meet ourselves, and God, and we discover the wonder and implications of being part of God's family.

Like this book, Robert's own life overflows with what it means to be fully human, made in the splendid image of God. Like Robert's life, this book is about the joy and wonder of the things that sustain us and challenge us along our spiritual path: love, compassion, mercy, justice, and endless hope.

I first met Robert in the 1970s in South Africa. His work against apartheid had opened his eyes and heart to the sacredness of every person. He struggled with whether to support apartheid by serving in the South African military or to refuse such service and be imprisoned. When he made the decision to not serve, we helped him leave South Africa.

Through the years, I've admired Robert's compassionate ministry of God's love and hope and the integrity of his life and leadership throughout many decades. It is a joy to see that authenticity revealed in these pages, inviting others into a deeper, transformative life with God. It is a humdinger of a book!

In a time of unprecedented global and local changes, leaving many feeling dislocated or wondering how to make a difference in the world, this book will become a timeless resource in your spiritual quest.

In a time when many hungrily search for values and meaning, this book will repeatedly inspire and draw you deeper and deeper into a spirituality of love and compassion for Creation, the human family, and yourself.

In a time when some people invoke the mantle of religion to divide and destroy, this book is a reminder of the God of Love who existed before religion.

Brimming with the hope and trust that God places in us, *A New Way to Be Human* is a must-have for anyone on a spiritual path—a timely reminder of what is essential to our journey: that God longs for us to be people of love and compassion.

Together with Robert, I ask: What footprint will you leave in this world among the rest of God's family and the fragile beauty of Creation?

We cannot each do everything, but this book reminds us that we can each do something, as partners with God.

The Most Reverend Desmond Mpilo Tutu
Nobel Peace Laureate
Archbishop Emeritus of Cape Town

Introduction

There is a new way to be human. There has to be, because our lives are at stake.

In the old way of being human, the global economy, global conflicts, and the seismic shifts of social media and technology result in uncertainty, anxiety, and apprehension about the unknown. The old way accepts the cynicism of the world with a resigned, bystander-victim mentality about life. The old way of being is built on compromises, resulting in choices that compartmentalize your life and keep you from being authentically you. In the old way, spirituality soothes your yearnings but keeps you sedated on a stunted journey that ignores much of what life has to offer. Your life is deeply affected by the old way.

And yet, you have a choice.

Your unique humanity is part of the spiritual fabric of the entire human story. In fact, the Holy yearns for you to be 100 percent alive and profoundly authentic, because without your full participation, those who need you most will miss out on what only you can give.

What if you quit accepting life as it is, and stop settling for so little? What if the world really can change? And what if that change begins with you?

Through the years, I've revisited this challenge, these questions, again and again. And my life—as well as the world around me—has been radically transformed in response. That's why I'm sharing my story. And that's why I offer this invitation to you.

As you step beyond the enclosures of your life, you will see the hairpin curves that life throws your way as opportunities to go deeper into who you are and to experience your journey as proactive engagement with the Holy and the world. In the process, you will find that all of life is bundled and mixed together. Your appreciation of your belovedness and your resulting delight in life is not a personal treasure for you alone, but a gift in transforming and polishing the world. In your oneness with others, you will experience a new resonance in being human. The arc of your story—of all that has made you unique—will reveal spiritual truths about the Holy in your life, egging you on to discover how your stories connect to the stories of those whom you might least expect.

You can experience this new way of being human by your willingness to do the work that transformation offers. The old way of clutching at and accepting a compromised life will give way to a life marked by vibrancy, gratitude, and authenticity about who you are. You will discover a new tenderness toward yourself, resulting in a renewed way of engaging with others and the world.

This book offers seven spiritual pathways to becoming fully alive. Each chapter explores a different pathway. Within each chapter, I share my story, and offer three practical stepping stones to help support your journey. At the end of each chapter, I offer a resting point for reflection and practicing what you've learned along the way.

Make the most of this book by approaching it—and your life—with unclenched hands and an open heart and spirit. The stories that I offer from the arc of my life are here so that you will also discover the Holy at work in surprising ways in your story. Awakened to this truth, you will begin to integrate the seven pathways offered into the whole cloth of who you are. Within each of the seven pathways, you will discover the three stepping stones clearing the path ahead for you. Your own truth-telling about the life you have, and the life intended for you, will allow you to experience these pathways as life-giving and life-changing.

The questions posed throughout this book are designed to awaken you to the magnificence of being deeply at one with yourself, the Holy, and others. If you have a trusted circle of spiritual pilgrims with whom to share this book, the pathways and stepping stones offered will become soul food for group discussion and learning.

So what will you choose?

Are you ready to join me on an unfolding journey to an integrated life grounded in compassion, love, and mercy? Will you let go of tinkering around the edges of your life and enter into a new consciousness of your relationship with yourself, those you love, the Holy, and the Universe?

The choice is yours. This prayer is mine: that the journey that brought you thus far—and the one that lies ahead—will be revealed as sacred ground, and that no matter where you start, you will finish well.

Yours for the journey,
Robert V. Taylor

My life is my message.
—Mahatma Gandhi

Pathway One:
Connecting Stories

Desmond Tutu's eyes twinkled as he leaned in with a simple, yet profound question: "Tell me about your life, Robert—not what you've done, but who you are." It was our first meeting. At the time, I was 22 years old. He was 49. I was a white South African young adult trying to figure out who I was. He was a black anti-apartheid activist and priest, considered public enemy number-one by the South African government at that time. I had been involved in anti-apartheid work for only a few years and felt privileged to be in his presence. What could we possibly have in common? I reflected for a moment. The best starting place for expressing who I was began with relating the transformative pain that shaped so much of my journey thus far, so I shared a story of my time in the hospital as a teenager. Little did I realize at the time the holy invitation Tutu was making, or the common ground we shared.

At the age of 15, my spine had grown out of place, forcing me to endure major spinal surgeries that lasted eight hours, followed by six weeks of lying flat on my back in a hospital bed. The pain was relentless. After each surgery, I left the hospital wearing a metal body brace for my upper torso that could not be removed—not even for sleeping or bathing. My classmates had to help me to classes and carry my books to school. All contact sports were forbidden. Experiencing these constraints at such a young age brought me face to face with the fleeting nature of life and unfolded a depth of awareness in me beyond my years. God redeemed the confines of my physical life to awaken a fire in my soul.

At the same age, I also began attending the school at the Anglican Cathedral in Cape Town. There I discovered my first sustained encounters with organized religion through the services we attended in the Cathedral each week. The soaring architecture of the space captivated me. I was engaged by the music and preaching. Yet it was the true-life examples the clergy used to illustrate the divisiveness, injustice, and violence of apartheid that changed me and awakened me to the power of story. As a result, I became a voracious reader, devouring every book about apartheid that I could get my hands on. I wanted to discover the truth about my country.

During my hospital stays, the school chaplain visited me and gave me a copy of *Naught for Your Comfort*, a book by an Anglican priest and monk named Trevor Huddleston. Published in 1956, two years before I was born, the book was the first systematic rejection of the theological framework with which the government justified apartheid. Huddleston offered a more expansive way of being human than apartheid imagined. As a typical 15-year-old South African white boy who had met very few people who were not white, I was enthralled.

Stories of ordinary people illuminated Huddleston's writing. In those stories, I met people from a place called Sophiatown, the lively, thriving community that Huddleston served as a priest. Because Sophiatown's multi-racial and multi-ethnic reality did not conform to apartheid's worldview of injustice and division, it was to be bulldozed. Surely this story was not about the same country that I lived in. Why hadn't I been told the stories that Huddleston shared? Transfixed, I read the book three times.

The luminous compassion and love of Huddleston and his community blazed brightly against the harsh ugliness of the bulldozers. Delight, dignity, justice, and compassion all shone through the pages. The stories of those in the book pointed to a hopeful resilience that could never be silenced, a radiant memory that could never be diminished or erased. As I lay in my bed dependent on others to help me with the simplest of daily routines, I understood Huddleston to be pointing to the interconnection of all life. His message served as my personal invitation to be born anew with compassion and humanity—to be more fully human, more fully alive.

In the fourth week of bed confinement and recovery, I woke up in the middle of the night attempting to sleepwalk. It was a terrifying moment. With legs unsteady from bed rest, I fell to the floor, sending my IV stand crashing to the floor. One of my roommates rang the bell for a nurse, who gently helped me back into bed and positioned me flat on my back. An hour later the same nurse returned to check on me. In the darkness she heard my gentle sobbing. I was frightened. Life suddenly seemed very bleak.

Off my nurse went at 2 a.m. and came back with hot chocolate. Together she and I sipped from steaming mugs, describing in hushed tones our favorite memories and our greatest hopes. She asked me about those who visited me in the hospital. As I described school friends, family, and the school chaplain, I told her that there were not enough visits. The hospital's limited visiting policy felt isolating. And then I said to her, "But I've had another kind of visitor." I described Huddleston and introduced her to the people I'd met through his stories. By then we had drained our mugs. I thanked her for her visit and said, "My own life doesn't seem as bad or terrifying as the lives of those who faced a bulldozer at their front door."

She smiled. On her way back to the nurses' station she said, "Mr. Huddleston has been a very good visitor."

As I paused in the telling of my story, Desmond Tutu's laughter filled the room, bringing me back to the present. Incredulous, I just looked at him, waiting for him to settle down. Finally Tutu said, "When I was a young boy, I had tuberculosis. I spent months in the hospital, just like you, lonely and afraid. Trevor Huddleston was my priest! He visited me almost every day, reading stories and talking to me. Huddleston inspired me to think about being a priest."

❧ ❧ ❧ ❧ ❧ ❧ ❧ ❧ ❧ ❧ ❧ ❧ ❧ ❧ ❧ ❧ ❧

Shared transformation, decades apart. If Huddleston had not visited each of us in his own way, sharing his vision of love through stories of Sophiatown, where might Tutu and I have ended up instead? Our common ground became holy terrain. Our mutual passion to end apartheid—engaged with the efforts and humanity of others—eventually changed the world.

⚜

On the common ground of our connecting story, Tutu then asked, "Tell me your thinking about serving in the military."

I shared with him my willingness to go to prison indefinitely—even at the age of 22—as a consequence for refusing to report for duty for the two years of service in the South African military that was compulsory for all white males. "I know I'll be given an office job because of my surgeries, but it would still be supporting the military enforcement of apartheid, which I am not willing to do," I explained.

Tutu thoughtfully said, "There will be a time when this kind of action will be important. It isn't now." I hadn't expected this reaction to a decision I had wrestled with for years. I had 30 days before showing up to report for military duty or else refuse to serve and be jailed indefinitely. Tutu said, "I'll put a call in to my friend Hays in New York. He is a priest and the rector of St. James Church. We'll get you out of the country and you can go to seminary in the United States." This was not what I had expected. The common ground of a connecting story was now common ground for an unexpected journey that would shape the remainder of my life.

A few days later, Tutu called me and said, "Hays told us to give him your flight number and someone from his church in Manhattan will meet you at the airport. Hays and his wife, Linda, will put you up in their apartment." I was reeling from the news and wondering how all of this could be arranged so quickly. Tutu added, "You'll need to get your academic transcripts to Hays immediately. There's a man at the U.S. Embassy in Cape Town who could send them in a diplomatic pouch."

Ten days after that call, I was at the airport in Cape Town surrounded by my parents, my brother, a cousin, and two friends wishing me farewell.

My grandmothers were seated on either side of me as we posed for a photograph. It would be the last time that I saw them alive. I tried to contain my own apprehensions about the unknowns that lay ahead. What were Hays and Linda like, I wondered? I had never been out of Africa, and New York sounded like a completely different world. Would a seminary accept me as a student? How would I support myself? And then the announcement came, "The flight to Rio De Janeiro is now boarding." Our farewells were bittersweet, charged with emotion as we hugged one another before I headed toward the gate to make the journey to an unknown land.

On the flight to Rio and on to New York, I marveled at the turn my life had taken. I couldn't imagine why Tutu had been so generous and clear about the path ahead when the journey looked so wildly unfamiliar to me. I reflected on the holy ground of how my story connected me to Tutu, and connected the two of us to Trevor Huddleston and the greater anti-apartheid movement. Our stories were opening a pathway to even greater possibilities.

⁍

We are each the author of our own story. Desmond Tutu's self-awareness of how his story continually shaped who he is infused him with a curiosity and desire to know who I was as an individual, versus what I had done. His invitation to tell my story catalyzed for me a lifelong journey of discovering and re-discovering that our stories matter. If I had not chosen to tell him what shaped me, we may never have discovered the unexpected intersection of life that transformed us both. With his invitation, he honored me as much as he honored the Holy interwoven into my life.

This book is my way of extending the same invitation to you.

⁍

Stories reveal common sacred ground for meeting your deepest self and others, inviting you onto unexpected terrain while shifting and shaping the journey that lies ahead.

Three stepping stones on our journey guide us into the pathway of connecting stories as we embark on the journey to becoming more fully alive.

1. *Share your story and the holy truth it reveals about who you are and who you are becoming.*
2. *Accept the invitation to live your story in connection with others.*
3. *Engage in intentional, mindful, everyday feasting with one another.*

Stepping Stone One: Share Your Story

Sharing your story reveals the Holy present in you, speaking through your story to yourself and others. If, on the other hand, you choose not to share your story, you choose to dishonor, devalue, and disbelieve the truths that your life reveals. A crucial element of your journey, sharing your story frees you to be human in a new way. As you engage in story-sharing, a new intentionality about life will emerge and result in relationships and work that bring you alive. Sharing your story begins with attentive listening, inviting self-compassion, and eventually connecting your stories to those of others.

Cultivate Attentive Listening

Attentive listening to your own stories as well as those of others reveals the presence of the Holy on your journey to becoming fully alive, and renegotiates the boundaries that frame how you see yourself—and others.

I wasn't always willing to listen to or share my story. In the culture of my childhood, claiming my voice or trusting my imagination was frowned upon. Great value was placed on reticence or silence. Reflecting upon how my own story might be cause for celebration was not an option, as those who told their story were viewed as inappropriately drawing attention to themselves.

When I arrived in New York, I did not feel comfortable self-disclosing in the way Americans did. I found myself speaking more about the "what" of South Africa than about my own journey. I assumed that my story was uninteresting, insignificant, and of little real interest to others. When pressed to tell more of my story, I felt uncomfortable and afraid. I wondered if I would sound self-absorbed. Then I began to appreciate that those asking for more were usually, like Tutu, asking who I was. I also realized that knowing and practicing my story allowed me to move beyond the fear that I would somehow lose part of myself. With each telling, I became even more comfortable, revealing the experiences that shaped my understanding of life, and in the process I discovered that instead I was meeting myself in a new way.

Had I remained captive to my fears, they would have compounded and grown in strength—much like a demon to be domesticated. In naming and calming my fearful anxiety, I opened a new pathway to the power of connecting stories. Just as Tutu engaged me with his attention, I now did the same thing for myself by listening attentively to my own story. This led me to look beyond past experiences and turn to the core of what those experiences revealed.

The framework of my story included how—as a white teenager—I came to terms with my physical constraints even while discovering the shameful truth of how apartheid intentionally denied the humanity of others. As I listened to my story, my passion surfaced with increasing force, revealing to me that love and compassion are central to our being, and that the sacredness of each person and our oneness as people serve as a guiding compass of life. The despair I experienced because of my spinal surgeries—not unlike the despair of apartheid—birthed a rare hope amid the most hopeless of circumstances. And I have discovered along the way that others have shared similar experiences.

Claire, a participant in a workshop on connecting stories, said, "I've done significant inner work over the years preparing me to become at ease with the many facets of Claire, and yet I've been ignoring this yearning to connect my story to others for a long time out of hesitancy and fear." Claire had been captive to her own fears of what the stories might reveal to her and to others. "I was terrified that my stories would have me at the edge of a cliff and that the reaction of others would make me lose my footing and fall over." Then she added, "The cumulative guilt I absorbed from my childhood religion infused me with a sense that I was never good enough and that my stories were prideful sin." The vestiges of guilt she left behind were revisiting her at a juncture in her life when she was ready to step away from their hold.

Claire knew that her journey invited her attention to the stories that shaped her path. Naming the resurfaced guilt diminished its power, making way for Claire to identify the Holy at work in her stories and in those whose lives were intertwined with hers. She began to more freely and spontaneously tell these stories in safe settings, delighting in the surprise that each story was more than an individual story. Claire was now free to tell stories as well as attentively listen to the truths and wisdom revealed in each one. The result has been a freedom to reveal her heart to others, thereby giving permission to others to reciprocate. "My relationships are deepened and my willingness to discover the Holy in others is alive each day," she says. At ease with the magnificence that her connecting stories reveal, Claire now lives with the truth that the Universe and the Holy reveal their wisdom through connecting stories.

Likewise, the multifaceted you revealed in your connecting stories will weave an authentic connection and carve out a new way of being human in the world.

Invite Self-Compassion

In knowing my story, I had to admit to three things: I disliked the truth that my whiteness created a privileged cocoon in which to experience life in South Africa, I felt shame that I had not responded earlier to the truths of that country, and I regretted not having done even more within the anti-apartheid movement.

By publicly telling my story, I invited people from their love and compassion to connect with and act on the stories I told about life under apartheid. It was also time for me to respond to the invitation of compassion by practicing it toward myself. My own story would be constrained if I allowed my dislikes, shame, and regrets to become defining.

Likewise, you will discover that sharing your story will reveal to you elements of your life that you cherish, as well as elements of life that cause you to feel shame. Every element of your story belongs to you. Although some details may not be appropriate or safe to include as you tell your story, you still need to know, name, and acknowledge the parts of your story that scare you, so that they do not imprison or constrain your journey. When you live with dislike, shame, or regret as a powerful force in your story, it creates a murky light for your journey, making it challenging to see the path ahead. Being compassionate and gentle about those things changes how you know and tell your own story. As you befriend your story and invite self-compassion, the shame-filled and painful elements lose their power to diminish you.

My friend Gwen describes it this way: "I'm a recovering alcoholic celebrating 15 years of sobriety, but I wasn't always able to be compassionate with myself for the stupid things I once did."

Gwen described the night when she hit rock bottom. It was a wake-up call. " I had been drinking and I passed out in the parking lot of a supermarket late one night. I was so gone that I could not manage to get myself up off the ground. I lay there for five hours." As we listened to Gwen describe her journey through the steps of Alcoholics Anonymous and acknowledging a Higher Power, her calm radiance enveloped us, offering no clue about the turmoil she once lived with as an active alcoholic, or the disruption and pain she had inflicted on others, including her son.

We were standing talking in a room in Cleveland where the homeless were served breakfast. Gwen volunteered there several times a week along with her son and his partner, both of whom are also recovering alcoholics. She said, "Whenever one of our homeless guests talks to a volunteer about their struggles with substance abuse they bring one of the three of us over to talk about our journey to sobriety. At first the guest usually does a double-take, because the three of us look like successful, comfortable, middle-class people."

Gwen's journey to live with self-compassion is still evolving and she makes a daily intention at the start of each day to be compassionate to herself and to those she meets. "I am awake to the engagement of the person

I'm talking with. At first they react to the fact that their assumptions of who I am can't be pegged by my appearance. At some point they ask how I came to love myself in spite of my story." Then Gwen added, "It's not in spite of my story; it's because of my story. It's in the blemishes and the falling down that I've learned to look more deeply into myself and discover the Holy. I believe the Holy wants us to be tickled pink about living with self-compassion."

Like Gwen, when you integrate your self-compassion and story, you allow yourself to move beyond getting caught in the potholes that have tripped you up along your journey. The result is freedom to listen to where your story invites you to place your energy, hope, and love. You become free to connect with your heart's passion. Being free is important, because the wonder of your story is desperately needed within the human family.

Connect Your Story

As you listen attentively to your story and invite self-compassion, your core values and passion are revealed. And as you intentionally live out your passion and values, the telling of your unique story offers a meeting place of the heart like the one that Desmond Tutu and I discovered.

As I became more comfortable in knowing and sharing my story, a new zeal for welcoming the stories of others emerged. I found myself listening and entering into the stories of others with the same attentiveness and compassion that I had developed for my own story. My engagement with life was suddenly richer. I began to hear and experience the Holy at work in the connection invited by this mutuality of story.

When your story connects your life to those of other people, you become liberated from a narrow consciousness of who you are. Your story becomes woven together with the truths revealed in the stories of others. Knowing and sharing your story is not simply a personal treasure. As you connect your story, you enter into a field of discovery shaping and integrating the journey you are on.

In the years after I first began sharing my story and inviting self-compassion, I began to connect my story to others. I spoke at universities and religious institutions, inviting people to enter into a common humanity acted on by a shared involvement to end apartheid. I wrote op-ed pieces for major newspapers, highlighting apartheid's denial of humanity. More than an exercise in self-awareness, connecting my story illuminated a path to me about being intentional in response to the larger truths that my experience revealed.

Richard and I met to explore the "desert land" of his journey. On the surface, his life path appeared to be one of sparkling success. At first he was only able to tell stories in an understated way that affirmed the successes of his professional persona. He admitted feeling trapped by the narrative that he told.

Like many men of his age, Richard was uneasy speaking about any of the emotions of his life. He was astounded as he sat with me one day crying as he said, "My family and even God will think less of me if I'm not successful; I live with constant fear that they will not love me unless I keep achieving." Amid his sobs he continued, "I've turned God and my family into tyrants; it's all my doing."

Richard began to connect with the painful truth that his life had been shaped from childhood by having to earn the love and praise of his parents. He said, "I'm only now realizing that the need to feed that narrative has been exhausting!"

Instead of accepting the inevitability of continuing to live in such a way, Richard began to make small but significant choices that allowed space for transformation. His wife expressed relief about his new awakening and actively encouraged his narrative of being authentically Richard. "The emptiness I had created through my singular narrative of success began to give way to a new awareness of my place in the world," he said. In telling stories that revealed his passions and yearnings, Richard began to understand that they revealed his increasingly authentic self.

As you share your story, invite self-compassion, and connect your story to others, you will learn to trust your story and integrate it into the many aspects of your life. A new way of being human emerges as you honor your story and the story of others. Like Richard, when you are ready to learn from your story, your life will reveal transformative invitations to connect your story with the fullness of who you are intended to be. You become more fully alive through the new choices available to you, and the world is never quite the same.

Stepping Stone Two: Accepting the Invitation

When you are secure in your own story, you discover that the stories of others offer you an invitation. As you accept these invitations, the vibrancy of the Holy at work infuses your life as you love, live, and celebrate your connection with others. Transformation happens. And the grounding of your own life is never the same again once you discover who you are in the context of the world around you. Accepting the invitation begins when you embrace curiosity, are grateful for who you are, and trust the new freedom that acceptance brings.

Embrace Curiosity

Embracing curiosity engages you in shaping a human story larger than your own. Old assumptions, hurts, prejudices, and hatreds—known or unknown to you—are changed in this new spaciousness. Core values become enlivened as connecting stories with others invites you to the journey of becoming fully alive. Different from nosy ferreting of information or intellectual show-and-tell, curiosity is soul food for your journey. It begins as you proactively approach each day mindful of others, and awaken yourself to what will be revealed.

As a teenager, I led a youth group in a rare, multi-racial South African congregation. The landscape of my world shifted as I entered this privileged circle of trust and accepted the invitation to enter into the stories of others. I saw families forcibly evicted from their homes and resettled in distant areas. They could have joined a congregation in the strictly segregated areas where they had been relocated. Instead, they chose to commute long distances to their home parish church, where family memories resonated and their spirit would not be assailed.

At our youth group barbeque, I soaked up stories from the host family of how three of their children left South Africa in order to freely practice their chosen professions as doctors and attorneys. Listening with attentive curiosity to what it meant to be denied the right to work freely in your vocation humbled and awakened me. As I listened to these stories of disruption—especially from other teens in the group—I wondered if I would have the self-worth and spiritual stamina needed to resolutely resist the government's attempts to dehumanize. I turned to my friend Muriel and asked if any of her family had left for similar reasons. In that moment, the sparkle of a teenage romance began. We were soon holding hands. This innocent adolescent gesture was fraught with questions of what it meant to cross a racial line vigorously enforced by the authorities. Reality quickly settled in as Muriel and I began to date. Our friends and family all looked kindly on our dating, but expressed concern that we were committing a criminal offense. Muriel and I could not legally swim at the same beach, attend a movie together, share a meal in a restaurant, or ride public transportation together, so our dates were spent at her family home or that of a clergy friend. An otherwise ordinary teenage romance became clandestine as we brushed up against the law.

Discovering this truth about my country felt like a crushing blow to the head—and heart. However, the confining prejudices of apartheid were no match for the curiosity and friendship of two lives woven together through connecting stories. Our very different stories and experiences of the same country engaged my curiosity. Our friendship, forged in a shared faith community, revealed a connecting story of common hopes, aspirations, and spirituality. Muriel and I were engaged in a human story that was larger than us, revealing a more spacious journey of being fully alive.

At a church I spoke at, I was intrigued by the invitation that one of the members issued to the congregation. Gloria spoke about the suppers called One Family Dinners that the congregation served to about 40 homeless people each week. She said, "While we always need people to set-up, cook, clean, and clear-up, what we really need is this: we need the gift of your presence as a family member sitting and sharing in a meal with our guests." She added, "No single act is more important than sitting down with a guest and listening."

As we spoke, Gloria expressed the reality of many volunteers. She said, "I'm really good at doing, at being busy. I organize and get the job done! But to sit with another human being and simply be present is a whole new experience for me." She explained that she had never seen this as "work" nor understood its significance. "I've always found it easier to serve than to sit." In taking on the new work of sitting in companionship with another person, Gloria paid attention to the curiosity she discovered in getting to know another person whose story and experience was beyond her usual realm of acquaintances. Embracing curiosity, Gloria discovered a mutual curiosity unveiled through connecting stories shared over a meal.

The result for Gloria is that her skills at serving and leading have been infused with new energy because of the curiosity of getting to know another person each week from among the guests at the One Family Dinners. The gift of being present has sharpened her belief that we are made for oneness with other people.

Embracing your curiosity through connecting stories is a journey of delighting in the life and wholeness of each person, including yourself. As you live and love your connection with others, you are transformed to a broader, deeper consciousness, illuminating your path to a new way of being human.

Grateful for Who You Are

Beware: Cultivating curiosity and living each day with gratitude for connecting stories will raise questions for your journey. Free of a narrow consciousness, your compassion and kindness will draw you to respond to the world with actions that meet the needs of others. This is not just "good works." Out of these actions flow personal fulfillment that fuels your journey, inviting you into new, life-shifting questions about who you are in relation to yourself and others.

In retrospect, my illuminating relationship with Muriel was also juxtaposed by irony. Even as I embraced curiosity about the constraints of apartheid and the lives of others, I allowed my paralyzing fear of being gay to banish the possibility of embracing a life-giving curiosity about my own sexuality. My lack of maturity at that time and my genuine affection for

Muriel notwithstanding, I am reminded of how easy it is to embrace curiosity with one arm and with the other to hold curiosity away from those truths that frighten me.

As I grew and matured, my curiosity to discover the truths of South Africa eventually led me to ask myself, "What does a spiritual life of integrity look like in response to such truths?" And yet as I began to respond to that question, I could not escape the gnawing question of "What does this mean about living a life of integrity about who I am?" The terrifying epiphany: Embracing curiosity about my life was also an invitation to live with wholeness—including my sexuality—and to be grateful and accepting of who I am. Gratitude for who I am took me beyond acceptance. It revealed to me that *I am* my brother or sister, and that I should live each day accordingly.

Your life and spirituality is never just about you. When you feed the hungry, tutor a child, provide access to art, or affirm the dignity of another person, your consciousness will shift, and in some small way, the world changes. Does this mean that I am meant to be my brother or sister's keeper? No. To be the keeper of another human being leaves little room for discovering your oneness with others, because "keeping" another does not allow for the mutuality that you discover in connecting stories.

Instead, I have discovered that the person with a need of some kind is actually just like me—a full, complex, loving, infuriating, and magnificent person. Like me, she or he wants nothing more than to be fully alive. Like me, she or he reveals the radiance of the Holy. Instead of being a "keeper" of someone else, in a way, I am my brother or sister.

This critical nuance was revealed in Desmond Tutu's disarming, grand laughter as I told him who I was. His curiosity erupted in delight over how the holy alignment of our personal journeys transcended the difference in our age, our skin color, and the vast difference in our upbringing. In that moment, he saw that we belonged to one another, and that my well-being was as important as his own.

But what of those who seem ungrateful for who they are and their unawareness of their magnificence so needed by the world? Israel was part of a staff team having photographs taken for inclusion in the organization's annual report. After the photographer took his photo, he showed it to Israel on the digital camera and said, "What a beautiful photo of you!" "I don't think so!" Israel declared, adding, "I cannot remember ever seeing a beautiful photo of myself."

His comment shocked and bewildered his colleagues in the room. Many of them admired his complexion and his innate handsomeness. Israel seemed unwilling and unable to see any of it, and they suddenly understood why he had steadfastly refused to have his photo taken with colleagues in the past.

In the months that followed, his work partner Maya attempted to engage Israel about his self-esteem and the magnificence that others so readily appreciated about him. Skilled at his work, Israel was steadfast in his inability to be grateful for who he is, and Maya accepted that she could not engage Israel to become grateful for who he is.

Maya said, "I had to detach from trying to change how he sees himself. I could continue to love what I saw in him and offer intentions for his awareness to be transformed. One day he will be ready to greet the teacher who allows him to accept the invitation to be grateful for who he is."

Likewise, only you can do the work of being grateful for who you are, knowing that with each embrace of that truth you contribute to allowing others to shine in their own time and in their own magnificence. By the same token, your life-shifting questions, acts of kindness, and generosity invite you to reshape your boundaries. As you choose to live your life as if you are your sister or brother, your connection to and your role within the world around you shifts.

⚘

My friend Jean discovered this truth as she connected her stories to others. As a teenager she walked to her neighborhood church with a spring in her step, feeling proud of the new coat she was wearing. As she jumped over a low wall into the church parking lot, a man grabbed her, forcing a gag into her mouth. Trying to determine her age, he asked how old she was. She remembers her lie as he loosened the gag to hear her answer—"Eleven," she said, and then she screamed as loudly as she could.

The sexual predator released the gag saying, "If you look back I'll kill you." Jean ran with a speed she did not know was possible, racing across the parking lot and into the parish hall where she saw familiar people drinking coffee and chatting. Jean asked if anyone had heard a scream. "Oh, yes," several people said. "And what did you do?" she asked. "Well, nothing," was the response. Jean left, and never returned.

Jean is a documentary filmmaker telling the stories of people who are often invisible or unheard. Jean says, "I may have screamed into a void of no response, but we each have a scream, a story, or moments of laughter that connect us. My filmmaking skill helps tell the connecting stories because each story is somehow our story."

Accepting the invitation to knowing who you are as your sister or brother invites you beyond narrow or constrained experiences of yourself and life. Instead of being someone who visits the world, you are an active participant of interconnection. Your invitation is to shape the human story and be grateful for who you are.

Trust Your New Freedom

Grounded by embracing curiosity and being grateful for who you are, you will discover a new freedom—a freedom to accept invitations that connect you to others...a freedom of hope that spans culture, history, and time to build bridges of affection between people. This new freedom is a treasure to be shared as you take your next steps on the journey to becoming fully alive with others and the Holy. It is a freedom you can trust.

In 1992, Desmond Tutu joined me for festivities celebrating the 225th anniversary of the congregation I led in Peekskill, New York. Once a predominantly white and dwindling congregation in a racially polarized city, it had been transformed into a community of many races and cultures. Community meals celebrating the ethnic cuisine of members provided a safe space for stories offered around shared tables. And the previously narrow view of the congregation was transformed into an expansive connected one on a field of curiosity and trust. There Tutu and I were, years removed from our first connecting encounter, marveling at how the new spacious freedom that marked this community celebrated the life we discovered in the oneness of our journey.

Curiosity, gratitude for who you are, and appreciating the freedom revealed in connecting stories are a trinity of invitation that you can choose to accept or reject. On your journey from a narrow, constrained view of your life, be alert for the comments and actions of those who find your freedom unsettling to their own constrained view of others.

Your intuition is part of your spiritual DNA, part of the toolbox for your journey to being fully human. Andrea discovered this truth in an unexpected way. In spite of a busy professional and personal life, Andrea was trying on a new freedom to polish the world and make a difference. She joined the board of directors of an organization whose mission reflected her passion for preserving undeveloped forests in the Americas. Andrea was connecting the stories and insights she had received from indigenous peoples in Central and South America with her own story of growing up in a family that worked successfully to create urban parks in several cities in the United States.

The executive director of the organization regarded it as a coup to have someone of Andrea's background and profile on the board. Andrea discovered that her experience on the board of directors did not correlate with the board that had been described to her in the nomination process. Instead, it was rife with internal disputes. She steadfastly persevered with the hope that she could help change the board dynamics.

Andrea's aversion to disappointing others collided with her intuitive knowledge that her continued board participation was life-draining to her, distancing her from her passion for the organization's mission. Instead of ignoring her intuition, she listened to and trusted it. She resigned from the board and took a significant volunteer role representing the organization in the cross-cultural dynamics between a North American board and indigenous groups in several countries.

Trusting her new freedom, Andrea listened to her intuition, developed new compassion for the fears she relinquished of disappointing others, and created a new way to serve a purpose she believed in. Andrea's transformative work with the organization has resulted in connecting stories being honored as a way of changing and polishing the world.

As you move forward on your journey, be attentive to each word, giving thanks, and allowing your every thought and action with others to become a celebration of the Holy. Your response will reveal just how much you trust your new freedom, and where you have room to grow.

⚘

Throughout the course of several years, members of a Jewish and Lutheran congregation shared meals, stories, and educational opportunities together in a mutual desire to know one another better. As their stories connected, their love for one another grew.

One night, a phone call awakened the rabbi, alerting him that his synagogue was on fire. He rushed to rescue the Torah from the flames. As he stood watching the building burn, he thought about the upcoming observance of Yom Kippur, the holiest of holy days, and wondered how his members would observe it. He didn't have to worry. As soon as the Lutheran pastor heard the news, he offered his church to the rabbi's congregation for as long as they needed it. Overwhelmed with gratitude amid the ashes, the rabbi marveled at how far both congregations had come.

Several days later, accompanied by members of the synagogue, the rabbi went to the church to prepare it for their Day of Atonement. As they made their way into the sanctuary, they were transfixed, and then began to weep. The Lutheran church had removed the large cross that marked the focal point of the room—and their religion.

"We never imagined that you would do this," said the rabbi.

The pastor responded, "My congregation and I have learned over our meals and stories that our beloved cross has been used by some as a sign to persecute Jews. We asked ourselves whether our identity as Christians required us to keep it up while we share this sacred space with you. We decided we were free to take it down. We know who we are and we treasure our shared spiritual path."

Your new freedom will be revealed to you in surprising ways. As you learn to trust your new freedom and lean into the opportunities it provides, old assumptions will cease to confine your engagement with others. Your shared journey becomes sacred terrain, transforming your sense of self, others, and the Holy One.

Stepping Stone Three: Everyday Feasting—Engaging in Intentional Communion

Free of a narrow consciousness, connecting stories invite you to experience life as a feast—daily. Partaking in sustenance together, fully present with another, your journey will be punctuated by communion with others. These are the moments presented to you by life in which you engage with another person over a cup of coffee, a simple meal, or an end of the day beverage. Expect to feast by cultivating and appreciating time for feasting. Extend invitations to feast by becoming awake and proactive. Accept invitations to feast with expectancy and thankfulness.

Cultivate Awareness and Appreciate Time

Competing demands for your attention and time can consume your day and make everyday feasting opportunities easy to miss, and yet your response to these opportunities shapes how fully alive you become. Accomplishing work is a good thing. Making and receiving opportunities to feast is even better. The secret to being intentional about feasting is developing an awareness of feasting invitations and an appreciation of time as a sacred life-beat of your journey.

In the story I shared about sleepwalking in the hospital, the nurse who helped me back into my bed completed her required task. I was back in my bed, the intravenous tubes were working, and my spine appeared to be undamaged by my nighttime sleepwalking. She could have easily returned to her nurse's station and left it at that. Instead, she responded to a fearful teenager by returning with mugs of hot chocolate. We were feasting! Beyond calming my fears and drying my tears, our shared stories established a connection between us that drove out isolation. In the remaining weeks of my hospitalization, we continued to feast as her awareness met my willingness to receive this gift—a gift that will remain with me forever. And yet, giving and receiving these gifts requires a counterintuitive paradigm of time.

For years, my day was punctuated by 15- to 30-minute blocks of time, and unexpected visitors were viewed as intrusions on the flow of the day. Even as I regretted that my life was being managed with such rigorous precision, I felt driven to stay on task. Unexpected invitations to feasting either went unrecognized or were perceived as scheduling minefields. I've now chosen instead to allow a more natural dance between work goals, and appreciate time as an irreplaceable gift. Unexpected encounters with those who invite a feast of some kind are now experienced with appreciation and expectation. Extending feasting invitations to others has become part of the practice of my spirituality.

When you cultivate awareness and appreciation, you become what you practice. In the 1970s, Kolia immigrated as a child with his family to the United States in the last days of the Iranian Revolution. Of Tehran he says, "When there is food left over you never toss it in the garbage; you give it out to the street sweepers who are very poor, because you know that it is probably the only meal they will get." He knows that such an action in Los Angeles where he lives would be poorly received, "But in Tehran it is accepted as an act of appreciative sharing. It reminds me of how lucky I am for the life I live. As one of the fortunate ones who have enough to eat, it reminds me that much of the world does not share in that luxury."

Kolia describes his appreciation for the fusion of beauty and colors of the food he eats, and that he doesn't have to search for food in order to survive. He says, "I've learned to appreciate the few minutes in conversation with the street sweepers. It reminds me of our shared human story and my own need to be mindful at home in Los Angeles about how I use and consume food." Kolia's awareness and appreciation has resulted in becoming involved with a program for sustainable agriculture in East Africa that teaches farming practices designed to conserve the environment and increase the yield on food crops for local consumption. "It might not be a lot, but it affects how my story is at one with the human family and the environment." Kolia lives with thankfulness for his new appreciation and awareness knowing that what he practices is part of who he is becoming in a new expression of being human.

Likewise, Tutu's simple request decades ago invited me to a feast of unexpected communion, resulting in a lifelong, life-altering relationship profoundly impacting both of our lives. It is a gift for which I am grateful every day of my life.

What if you feasted daily? Whose life might be changed as a result?

Be Awake and Proactive

When you are intuitively awake to others, you invite a response. So as you begin to proactively engage in intentional communion, be mindful of the invitations you give and receive, and awake to how the Holy may appear.

Soon after I arrived at one congregation I led, a woman named Sheila began to withdraw from participation in church activities, and her attendance at services was sporadic. My repeated invitations and attempts to reach out to her throughout many years were met with a polite but resolute unwillingness to meet. Yet much to my surprise, there she was, unexpectedly knocking on the door. She seemed apprehensive.

I invited Sheila to come in and went to get some coffee for us. When I returned I noticed a small gift-wrapped box on the table in front of her.

Sheila said, "I've come to say I'm sorry. Thank you for welcoming me today, and thank you for your invitations over the years. I couldn't deal with you being openly gay. I've said terrible things about you." Tears began to roll down her cheeks as she added, "It's not about you. I've never been able to integrate my life story and I was envious and threatened by how you connect the dots."

She paused, taking a deep breath before continuing, "My daughter is gay, and I didn't know how to fit her truth into my life. The more I tried, the harder it was. I love her. It's not about her either. It's about me. My own image of my life has been a picture set in stone."

I thanked Sheila for her courage and her truth. She responded, "I'm letting go of the images that have chained me. I've begun to live into the truth of my life as it is. Thank you for helping me in spite of my being unresponsive and mean." As she reached for the small gift box she said, "This angel is a gift. Like angels, you and my daughter have helped calm my fears about myself." A simple response to Sheila's knock on my door inviting her in for coffee had turned into an unexpected feast and new communion for both of us.

Paulo discovered a different path to being awake and proactive as he reflected on how captive he had become to the high stress levels of his job. He noticed that he was eating lunch at his desk and turning to fast foods and high-sugar snacks for a quick energy boost. He said, "This is not how I want to live. I'm feeling disconnected from my body and my meditation practices have fallen by the wayside."

Facing a choice about practicing mindful living, Paulo began to build five-minute breathing breaks into his day. In a quiet space near his office he sits, paying attention to the breath flowing through his body. On some days, he does no more than be connected to the flow of his breath; on others he focuses on a word to meditate on.

The result has been a reduction in his stress levels and a reintegration with his body. Paulo attributes this to a renewed grounding in himself and a daily feasting with the Holy and the Universe that has emerged from his choices of being proactively awake.

In your daily life, be awake to invitations that present themselves, and be proactive in extending an invitation to feast over sustenance of some kind. As you trust your story and accept the invitation to connect with the stories of others, you create the space for everyday feasting and communion with those around you.

Expectant and Thankful

Expectancy and thankfulness are important steps toward preparing to receive invitations to feast. Your openness to the unexpected, transformative gifts of interaction that come your way reflects your willingness to journey with others and has the potential to set off a virtual tsunami of difference-making in the world.

After an early morning cardio workout at my gym, I headed to the exit, mentally running through a catalog of appointments and tasks to be accomplished in the workday ahead. As I waited for the elevator, a man whom I had spoken to on several occasions joined me and said, "I'd like to speak to a priest at your church." I gave him the phone number of the office saying, "One of the priests would be glad to meet with you." Heading to my car, it dawned on me, "He's asking to meet with me and he is not able to say that. I've just brushed him off."

I walked through the parking lot and found him getting into his car. I said, "Why don't we meet over lunch or tea?" Over lunch the next day I was privileged to enter into his story and his questions about making a life-changing decision. A brilliant, talented man was about to take the next steps on his journey to becoming fully alive. I was invited to take part—and I nearly missed it! Immersed in self-absorption, my expectancy level and awareness of the invitation being presented were dimmed. Thankfully, even though my grounding was off-kilter, the realization of what I was being offered finally kicked in, and I was able to respond before it was too late. As I left our lunch conversation offering gratitude for this unexpected everyday feast, my joy was made complete.

On your journey, cultivate expectancy that invitations to everyday feasting will present themselves to you. Expect that they will be part of becoming fully alive to the possibilities of life revealed in connecting stories. Beware of taking invitations for granted because you then lapse out of intentional awareness.

The scripture tells the story of Jesus's followers traveling from Jerusalem to the town of Emmaus. They were consumed with trying to make sense of the death and resurrection of their beloved rabbi. The story tells that Jesus joined them as they walked. Absorbed in grief, loss, and despair, the storyteller says that their eyes were not able to recognize who had joined them. Reaching their destination, they participated in a meal with the stranger who had walked with them. We are told that as they ate together, they realized who this was: "Their eyes were opened and they recognized him; and then he vanished from their sight."

Like those followers, your journey is marked by moments of not being expectant or thankful. At a family reunion, the children on the outdoor dance floor brought a scowl to Paul's face. "It's way too late for these kids to be up," he thought. He began running through a catalog of gripes about his perceived wrongs of modern parenting. Then he noticed a father dancing with his 5-year old son, and Paul was transfixed and surprised by the delight he witnessed.

Paul could have chosen to continue obsessing about his pet peeve. Instead, he allowed himself to enter the invitation presented by what he saw. "I began to notice other young children on the dance floor under the night sky surrounded by family. Their delight was palpable; how could I not enter into it?" he asked. As Paul stopped clinging to his litany of wrongs he noticed that his sense of obligation at attending the reunion began to shift. "Appreciating the joy of the dancing children and generations enjoying one another, I felt myself opening up. Much to my surprise, I was delighting in the evening!" he said.

The result is that Paul now lives each day with a mindful intention of expecting to be surprised by delight and relationships that express a joy of feasting. It is a spiritual practice opening up the landscape of his life.

On your journey to becoming fully alive, everyday feasting opportunities reveal the sacred ground of your journey with others. In the feast, a glimpse of the Holy will be revealed among you, opening your eyes to the stepping stones ahead. Your gratitude and thankfulness for each feast becomes a grounding part of your journey on a new way to being human.

Reflect:

- What step will you take—today—to share part of your story?

- Whose story have you listened to today? How has it changed your connection to yourself and others?

- What if you feasted daily? Whose life might be changed as a result?

❧ ❧ ❧ ❧ ❧ ❧ ❧ ❧ ❧ ❧ ❧ ❧ ❧ ❧ ❧ ❧ ❧

Spirited Practices

- Each day, name or write down something magnificent revealed in trusting your own story. Give thanks for trusting it. Journal if you feel inspired.

- Invite awareness of your journey and open your consciousness to the Holy and see what happens. How many connecting stories do you discover?

- Be aware and awake to the feasting opportunities that each day presents. Each night, reflect on what you have discovered on the field of feasting that day.

Only when we are friends with our selves—
all of our selves—can we take care of and
love one another.
—Thich Nhat Hahn

Pathway Two:
Breaking Through Enclosures

I was healed. The numbness in my lower body was gone. When I stood up, I could feel the ground beneath my feet. Stumbling to walk had given way to a new spring in my step. In accepting an invitation for prayers for healing, I wasn't sure that I even believed in the possibility of healing. Increasingly enclosed by paralysis in my body, my experience of healing set me free of the physical enclosure that my 16-year-old body had become. I was unprepared for the other enclosures that my healing would lead me to break out of.

I was a white boy raised in the dark days of apartheid in South Africa. Apartheid, the enforced separation of races in that country, was presented as the "will of God" by a government who used scripture to justify its violent and dehumanizing policies. God was invoked to support their belief in the superiority of white people over all others.

The meaning of apartheid—apartness—is a denial of the human quest for oneness. Apartheid attempted to enclose four racial groups, separating them from one another like cattle in pens. In 1974, at the age of 16, I was beginning to understand these enclosures designed to brutalize our humanity.

A religious experience had led me to attend a weekly Bible study at the home of the Anglican Archbishop of Cape Town, Bill Burnett. The chaplain to the Archbishop, Ivan Weiss, approached me at the end of a Bible study and announced, "We'd like to pray with you." I was startled by Ivan's words. As I looked quizzically at him he added, "We'd like to go in there to pray," pointing to the low doorway at the far end of the living room that led into a small chapel. I looked over Ivan's shoulder at the 70 people milling about the living room in Cape Town's oldest continuously lived-in home, which served as the official residence of the Archbishop. I felt relieved that the prayers being offered would be in a less public space than this imposing room.

I could still hear the ecstatic prayers and cheerful praise songs lingering in the air as the lanky, gaunt-looking Archbishop ambled through the room towering above everyone else. I felt anxious, apprehensive, and expectant about this prelate and his chaplain offering to pray for me. I'd never prayed with them alone before, it had always been in the safety of the crowd gathered each week. Were they going to exorcise me? Had someone revealed that I might be gay? Surely not, I thought. I was too busy hiding it to be talking about it.

As the Archbishop stooped over to put his arm around me, he led us into the chapel. In the evening light this small room seemed darker than ever. "Please kneel at the altar rail," he instructed me. He and Ivan stood, one behind me, and the other in front of me at the altar rail. I felt their hands pushing down on my shoulders as they began to pray, their baritone voices invoking the Spirit. As their voices quieted and the speech slowed, their hands moved, pressing down on my skull.

I tried to pry my head up to see their faces. All I could see was the crucifix on the wall in front of me behind the Archbishop. I had never experienced anything like this before. I wondered how long we'd been there praying. I felt a comforting warm sensation flow through my body. Then these two men put their hands under my arms and lifted me up to stand.

They had prayed for a physical healing of my spine after two unsuccessful surgeries had left me with increasing paralysis in my lower limbs. They both hugged me. "Your body is being healed," said the Archbishop. I didn't know how to respond to such an assertion. As we walked from the chapel through the living room, the Archbishop said, "Your body will not enclose you again." I wondered what on earth he meant.

In the weeks that followed, I realized I was no longer stumbling on the ground when I stood up. The numbness in my lower limbs had disappeared. I kept saying, "Thank you, God." My admiration for the Archbishop and Ivan was boundless.

As I walked into my orthopedic surgeon's office for a scheduled appointment, I was apprehensive about what his x-rays of my spine would reveal. Looking at them he said, "Your spine is an example of what our surgery can achieve. We're very pleased with what we see." Leaving his office my apprehension had turned into delight. I had a bounce in my step. I wanted to hug the Archbishop and God.

That delight must have shined through me at the next Thursday prayer meeting at the Archbishop's home. At the time of sharing personal stories I quickly chimed in with the story of the prayers for healing. "I keep being amazed that further surgery is not necessary. But I don't know what to make of the Archbishop's words about not being enclosed again."

George approached me at the end of the evening and asked, "Would you come to our church and tell your story?" He added, "Come for the weekend." Although I'd spoken to George and his wife Mary at several Thursday gatherings, his invitation was unexpected. I'd never visited a black community in South Africa before. Questions raced through my mind: "What would it be like to stay with George and his family? How should I respond to his request? What did I—at 16 years of age—have to say?" Before I could think about it further I said, "I'd love to do that, George." I had accepted an unexpected invitation to be healed, and now I was accepting an invitation that was even more unexpected. My life would be transformed by accepting both invitations.

❧ ❧ ❧ ❧ ❧ ❧ ❧ ❧ ❧ ❧ ❧ ❧ ❧ ❧ ❧ ❧ ❧

As I prepared for the visit, I felt anxious. I went to see Ivan and said, "I'm supposed to preach at two services. I don't know how to preach and I don't think I have a lot to say." He quickly offered, "Telling your story and listening to it will be healing. Be open to what will happen."

The next morning at George and Mary's church, my heart raced as I headed to the pulpit. Worrying about what I would say, I wondered if the zit on my chin would be distracting to the congregation. My hands felt sweaty as I held on to the podium. Looking out at the congregation I realized that I was the only white person in the church. A white teenager in the pulpit, no less! It was a new experience to be a minority for the first time. As I looked out at their faces, I wondered what they were thinking.

Everyone dressed as if they were attending an important function, making me grateful that I had worn the only tie I owned. I was beginning to understand that for many, church was the grounding event of each week, and with their attire they honored the importance of the Holy in their lives. As I began to speak, an intuitive sense of welcome flowed toward me from the attentive, hospitable crowd. We shared a common journey with the Holy. I felt no judgment. As I settled into telling my story of healing, I heard in my mind the words offered by the Archbishop about never being enclosed again. Was this weekend the path to a deeper healing?

As I finished my story, applause erupted. Embarrassed, surprised, and grateful at the unanticipated graciousness of the crowd, I broke out in a beaming smile. The courage to face my anxieties and apprehension about a foreign and unknown world had opened my life to the unimagined. The generosity of those clapping hands welcomed me to a vibrant canvas of life, and coaxed me into an experience of becoming more fully alive with others.

❧

By accepting this invitation into the unknown, I began—even as a teenager—to experience the pathway of breaking through enclosures.

What is an enclosure? Enclosures are self-fulfilling actions and beliefs that keep you from being who you are meant to be. When we allow ourselves to be confined by unacceptable expectations and boundaries drawn by others—such as family, culture, religion, and politics—we accept an enclosure, and so define a limited us.

When hiding behind your own particular enclosure, you choose to live with a cramped heart, a squelched voice, and often, a lack of compassion for yourself—and others. Although the choice to be enclosed can happen subtly through time, enclosure is no small thing. Your life is at stake! Enclosures lock you away from the fullness of joy intended for you by the Holy, and deprive the world of the gifts that only you can give—shielding you from the people who most need your influence.

The good news is this: Because we choose our way into an enclosure, we can choose to break out. Life presents us with such invitations each day.

In my own life and through my work with thousands of people, I have discovered three stepping stones that allow us to accept the invitation of opening that encloses us:

1. *Listening to our voice and discerning the voices of others—to encounter the Holy.*

2. *Becoming present to self—to see glimpses of the Holy in who we are.*

3. *Cultivating the way of compassion—to extend the love of the Holy to others.*

These simple truths orient our lives to the joy of living in a more spacious way than any enclosure can offer.

Stepping Stone One: Listening to Your Voice and Discerning the Voice of Others

The enclosure of apartheid South Africa was intentionally created to keep ideas and people walled off by creating and manipulating a fear of those who are different from us. Constructed on the foundation of diminishing the value of other human beings, this enclosure was intended to create the assumption that the voices of a few were more valued than the voices of each person.

Your voice is too important to be devalued in any way. Discernment about what voices to listen to is critical, moving you beyond codependent, life-draining experiences into fullness of life. Testing your voice is a spiritual practice for your journey. As you discern and test your voice and that of others, your voice frees you from enclosures, allowing you to cross through the lines that confine you to discover the Holy present in the voices of each person.

Discernment Is Critical

As I gave voice to my healing in that little South African church and listened to the voices of those whom the apartheid government wanted to silence, I found it impossible not to speak with my family about what I experienced. With the breathless discovery of a teenager, I shared my story at one family gathering only to be greeted with "You're treading on dangerous ground; you should be quiet!" and, "There's never smoke without fire; the government must know what it's doing."

I was discovering that it is often those closest to us who offer enclosure by broadcasting their bad advice—not because they are bad people, but because when we choose a path to new truths about who we are and how to exercise our voices, they feel threatened. When we make a choice to continue to grow on the path to a new way to be human, the anxiety level of those who choose to remain in their own enclosure increases. Ironically, the more you find your own voice, the more insistent those other voices can become. This is where discernment comes in. Who do we listen to? And who do we ignore?

Discernment is critical because unearthing our voices and becoming who we are meant to be leads us to our hearts' passions. As we make this journey, the voices of bad advice can dampen our passion as they flood in like a tsunami, shrouded in soothing tones about our welfare. Codependent urges kick in as we make apologies that they really "mean well" or "it's just their love for me speaking." In reality, such voices usually have little to do with us. Instead, these voices are a demand that we not upset their life or create an opening in their enclosure. Codependency does nothing to allow light to shine in our life or theirs.

Your voice is to be celebrated as a reflection of your individual magnificence. Your spiritual journey is about the breath of life flowing unstopped and unstoppable through you. Without breath you are voiceless, and without voice, you block the flow of the breath of life bringing you fully alive.

In a workshop I led on the pathways to becoming enlivened, one of the participants raised her hand toward the end of the day and said to the group, "I've had an unexpected epiphany that I'd like to share." Martha said, "I've spent years engaged in contemplative prayer practices. They've been a gift to me. But today I've felt like a bird breaking out of my shell learning to sing for the first time." The other participants leaned in listening to someone who was clearly not used to speaking in public.

Martha went on to talk about her practices saying, "I've always listened for the voice of the Holy somewhere out there," as she gestured with her arms to the space around her. "I'd never imagined what I was missing is the Holy in here," pointing to herself. Smiling broadly she added, "I feel as though I'm beginning to learn a new song. The notes and the lyrics have always been there, but I've never paid them any attention."

Testing Your Voice

Our own song, once recovered in us, is a gift of freedom opening a pathway to a more richly layered life. In the months that followed, I heard from Martha who kept testing her own newly reclaimed voice. She wrote saying, "I used to believe that my voice was insignificant and that it would be a selfish thing to pay attention to it. This was normal for me. As I trust my voice, I'm discovering that I listen to the voices of others with new ears. And I can discern which voices to ignore. My life has been like breaking out of a thousand egg shells since that moment of epiphany with you."

"I've begun to remember the voices from my childhood," said Martha. "Voices of those who loved me but who repeatedly asked me, 'Who do you think you are?' or, 'Why do you think such thoughts?' I'm realizing that the voice I'm appreciating as an adult is not a new voice. It's my voice unearthed after years of storage." The truth being revealed was the inverse of those questions that had resulted in putting her voice into a holding pen for decades.

We serve no one's happiness or life by trying to fix or mend. Detaching from those whose voices insist we fix or mend their lives is an exercise in affirming the humanity of all and the Holy present in each person. Each of us can only save the life we are responsible for: our own. By detaching emotionally and spiritually, we say to another person, "I love you; I want your happiness; I will be actively hoping for you to recover and claim your own voice and passion. Someday I pray we will celebrate our voices finding a new harmony."

As Martha's enclosures opened, she began to listen and engage with other people in a new way, unafraid of what their voices might reveal. On another occasion, Martha wrote to say, "For the first time I'm appreciating the Universe and the Holy in the voice of all kinds of people. My every encounter seems different. I'm appreciative, I'm learning, and I'm filled with anticipation about what I will hear."

But what if the structure of your daily life keeps you from familiar loving companionship with your own voice? Jacky participated in a multi-day retreat that I led, and on arrival announced that as thrilled as she was to be part of the retreat, she was not sure that she would make the daily morning meditations. "I just don't know if I can be quiet for 30 minutes," she offered.

Jacky was present for the first meditation and on the second day she arrived for it 15 minutes early. On the third day, each participant was invited to select a glass prayer bead from a cloth sack. Jacky's randomly selected meditation bead had the phrase "*Be Still*" etched into it. Afterward, she said to me, "This bead must surely have been meant for someone else! I start talking the moment I wake up in the morning and then my feet hit the ground running. I am constantly in motion, and I am still talking non-stop until my head hits the pillow in the evening. I don't know if being still is even a possibility for me!"

Without fail, Jacky was the first person to arrive at each ensuing meditation time always carrying her "*Be Still*" bead with her. Jacky could have chosen to write off the invitation of the experience that the bead provided. Instead, she was willing to see in it an invitation to a new practice. In being still, Jacky listened to her breath and said, "As I was doing this, I realized I was listening to my body for the first time. Some physical pain I had is gone. I'm aware of how loosened and relaxed I am."

The transformative insight came when Jacky acknowledged, "My life has been spent on the run with a torrent of words spoken incessantly. As I've practiced being still, I've received a gift of listening to my voice. I'm not sure what that means for me yet, but I'm beginning to love what it reveals in the stillness." Months later, I heard from Jacky, "I've discovered that my voice has oneness with my intuition and imagination. I'd never known that before. I keep testing it in small ways. I still talk a lot because that's me, but I'm no longer enclosed by the barrage of words."

Listening to and trusting your voice reveals truths about the unique person you are. Otherwise, you deprive yourself and the world of your place in the Universe. With each testing of your voice you accept the invitation to be a person of inestimable value.

Freeing Your Voice

As your own journey unfolds, everything you experience has the potential to open a gate to discovering more richly textured layers of what it means to be more fully alive. Martha or Jacky could have chosen to turn her back on that moment of epiphany in the workshop and return to the safety of a familiar enclosure. Instead of being captive to fear, anxiety, or the lure of the familiar, they each drew on honed resources of listening attentively, responding to an invitation to be transformed.

Listening to Martha and Jacky describe their journeys, I realized that I had developed a deeper appreciation for the enclosures opened up as a result of being asked to speak of my healing experience. With trepidation, surprise, anxiety, and delight, I recognized that my voice was drawing me toward a different light of new voices and away from my enclosure. I received courage and hope from those who allowed their voices to speak from their heart's passion. Companions like Mary and George were not nameless, faceless, or voiceless travelers on my journey. My experience of healing was intimately connected to the healing power of these new voices opening a door leading to a path of oneness among people.

❖ ❖ ❖ ❖ ❖ ❖ ❖ ❖ ❖ ❖ ❖ ❖ ❖ ❖ ❖ ❖ ❖

How did I discern the healing power of these new voices? First of all, it was clear that there was no expectation for their lives to be fixed by me. Instead, our voices became united with those of others in hope and love for the unity of all people. These are the marks of people who are practicing their voices in order to become wondrously human—and as we listen, we refine our intuition. Then the larger truths of compassion and happiness for all can be sung and worked for together. To pursue happiness for all people, we have to first claim and save the only life we are capable of saving— our own.

As I practiced my own voice and joined with these new voices, I gained greater discernment and recognized that the murky light of the voices of bad advice was glaringly different from the new voice I was trying on. The light on my path was doing more than illuminating the voice I was discovering as my own. As I tested and trusted my voice, it revealed that the Holy was striding along with me.

Freeing your voice is a recurring exploration on your journey to a new way of being human. With each new invitation, you plumb the depths and texture of your life and place in the Universe. With each expression of freeing your voice, you discover new truths about your values and the passion within you that brings you fully alive.

I once led a congregation in which the ordination of women was ridiculed by most of those in leadership positions. In the selection process, I had been clear that my position was markedly different and that I believed the full inclusion of women was an invitation to delight in the magnificence and work of one another, free of enclosures.

We engaged in a process that brought ordained women to preach and teach in the congregation. A series on the ordination of women culminated in a woman priest being the first woman to preside at a service of communion in that congregation. As the time for that drew closer, I received warnings from a few members that unnamed "people" would leave the congregation if I went through with this. A few angry people told me that many would refuse to receive communion and one person informed me that I would not "last long."

I wondered if my time in that congregation would be short-lived. Was I being threatened? I knew in my heart that a once-dwindling congregation beginning to rebound and grow had the capacity for change. My voice and intuition told me that unless we could be a community that celebrated the fullness of all people, we would have no possibility for new life and growth. This was not only a test of leadership and of the generosity of the congregation, it was also the claiming and freeing of my voice.

As Sunday approached, I wondered what my voice and words would convey. I named the truth that there were several reactions to a significant event. We spoke that day about who is invited to any table where the Holy is present or where communion of any kind is offered. One family chose to leave the congregation. Others worked through their reactions and remained active members. In the months that followed, a significant increase of new members occurred as people were drawn to a community where the voice and hopes of all were intentionally honored.

In reflecting on what happened, I realized that in freeing my voice, the voices of the congregation had been freed. Instead of choosing to remain in an enclosed pen that diminished the life of some, we embarked on a journey to trust, name, and delight in the magnificence of the Holy discovered in each person.

Whenever you unearth and trust your voice—for the first time or for the umpteenth time—it is cause for giving thanks, for celebration, and for gratitude. With each new epiphany, an enclosure opens inviting you to the work of transformation. Only you can keep the enclosure bolted shut or receive the opening as a gift. In accepting the gift, you choose a new way of being human.

Stepping Stone Two: Becoming Present to Self

We have each been told, "If only you were not...divorced, single, a woman, Latino, American, Iranian, rich, poor..." The person uttering those words draws an enclosure, cordoning off an essential part of you. When you buy into such words, you internalize their narrow rejection of your magnificence, tacitly conspiring to accept a confining enclosure that others have demarcated for you. By being present to yourself, you choose instead to discover the Holy bringing you alive as you are. Your life depends on this mindful grounding.

Grounded in Your Reality

A life-giving marker of your journey is to be present to yourself and the reality of your life at this particular moment, to acknowledge your enclosures for what they are, and to choose to break through them. All too often we live somewhere else—in our heads, instead of our hearts—wishing away the present, longing for the past, imagining the future, or expecting that another person will change our reality. Living this way adds another layer of enclosures to your life.

Enclosures can be literal, as well. Each spinal surgery I experienced as a teenager was followed by six months of living in the physical enclosure of a metal body cast. Suddenly, it seemed, everything in my life was organized around protecting my spine. My range of motion and natural body movement were restricted. Carrying weight of any kind was forbidden, so my classmates carried my books for me. Humiliated, embarrassed, and stripped of every last remnant of adolescent invincibility, the temptation to escape reality by focusing on "what is wrong with this picture" was great. Naturally, I spent most of my time impatiently longing for the cast to be removed.

One night in the quiet of my bedroom, I silently cried in despair of ever freeing myself from this devastating enclosure. My Black Labrador, Sheba, gently climbed onto the bed with me and laid down gingerly, as if she knew to be careful about my spine. She snuggled up to me delicately, showering me with licks of tender affection. By drawing me back into the moment with her, Sheba showed me that even within my physical enclosure, I was crying my way into an emotional enclosure of self-pity. Layer upon layer, I compounded my sense of physical restraint by unwittingly walling myself away from what was real, and in effect, conspired against my own freedom.

Eventually, I made a shift. My prayers from within my physical confinement became a time of releasing anxiety and impatience, giving me eyes to see that the classmates carrying my books were a gift, preparing me for moving beyond the enclosure. Embarrassment and resentment gave way to a new reverence for the fragility of life. Mindfulness about the beauty of a healing body tempered my impatience over my slow recovery. The enforced time of physical stillness provided me opportunity to accept the invitation to choose to be present to myself.

Accomplishment dissatisfaction is an enclosure that distances many people from being grounded in the truth of their lives. A woman named Sylvia said to me, "I feel like a petulant child saying this because my life is so full, but I experience a constant low-level dissatisfaction in my life. I always want to be accomplishing more; I want to make a bigger impact in the world. Why do I feel dissatisfied?"

Sylvia took inventory of her life and identified her playful and rewarding marriage as an anchor in her life. She was engaged in the lives of her children and was proud of them while her extended family was mostly a source of joy. Sylvia's professional accomplishments had been lauded and celebrated by her colleagues. As we spoke about this inventory, she said, "I don't think I've acknowledged or named this before, but ever since childhood I've been unsatisfied with what I've achieved; I've always believed I need to be a bigger player."

Faced by new self-awareness, Sylvia could have chosen to remain penned in by the lure of familiar dissatisfaction. Instead, she chose to move out of her self-enclosure and onto a previously unexplored new landscape. As she named and celebrated her relationships and accomplishments, Sylvia's awareness of her life began to shift. She realized that "I've spent a lifetime focusing on the next accomplishment and how to be more impactful. I've seldom been present to the things and people who ground me, including myself."

It is in Sylvia's DNA to accomplish and make an impact, and she now acknowledges this truth about who she is. The result of her awareness has her placing equal value on the life-giving relationships that nourish and sustain her, delighting in them as they are without the need to accomplish anything. She says, "I feel like I'm flourishing for the first time in my life. Accomplishments are not the only driving force of who I am. My drive is now in harmony with the things and people who ground my reality."

Harmony between seemingly opposite forces pulling at your life is possible when you are willing to become aware of the accomplishment dissatisfaction that you live with. Like Sylvia, it is possible to step beyond the enclosure of dissatisfaction when you are present to the reality of who you are.

Being present to yourself and the Holy is not about escaping the reality of your experiences in the present. Nor is it about forgetting, denying, or ignoring all that has made you who you are. Like the journey itself, becoming present is an ongoing process. It is an invitation to a new way of being human, replete with many refusals and acceptances. It is part of your response to becoming fully alive.

Showing Up for Life

The African concept of Ubuntu says that "I am only a person in the context of other people. I am only human because you are human and your humanity affirms mine—without that there is no wholeness." Showing up for life invites you to develop an intentional rhythm of being aware of the richly textured layers of past experiences that accompany you in any given moment on your journey, while being simultaneously grounded in the surprises of the present. You will discover this gift by walking with those who transform your understanding of being present.

I met Clifford at a center providing services for immigrants. He had volunteered there for several years but wondered, "What good does it do showing up here each week? I can't measure my impact." I asked him what it meant to the people served by the center to have him present. A few weeks later he called to say, "One of the guys at the center thanked me; in broken English he said the men looked forward to me being there every Friday." Clifford could easily have brushed the comment aside. Instead, he accepted it as a gift, as an invitation to reconsider how he showed up for life. He said, "I've discovered that my compassionate presence is just as important as my goal-driven career."

❖ ❖ ❖ ❖ ❖ ❖ ❖ ❖ ❖ ❖ ❖ ❖ ❖ ❖ ❖ ❖ ❖

A New Way to Be Human

But what if you are physically removed from being present in the way that you would like to be? Following the devastating tsunami of 2011 in Japan and the unfolding disaster for the Japanese people, my friend Carlene, who lives in a small isolated rural community, called to say that she was riveted by the coverage she was watching on television. "My heart aches at what I see. I want to do something, but I feel helpless and physically isolated from joining others. I'm struggling with my outrage at those who claim this disaster is the judgment of God."

Instead of remaining enclosed by her feelings of outrage and helplessness, Carlene chose to create space for her compassionate response. She learned of a spiritual community across the country that was holding a daily vigil for the people of Japan, at the hour of their vigil she joined them in spirit via a video link and offered her prayers and intentions alongside those of others. She sought out stories of those responding to the upending of lives in Japan, sharing them in person in her local community and with a wider geographic circle of friends through social media. She actively used these tools to invite people to financially support relief efforts. As Carlene updated me on her response, she said, "I feel a new oneness with those who are trying to cope and rebuild that has placed me in a far more expansive circle than the boundaries of the rural community I live in."

The result was that Carlene's heart was opened in compassionate oneness with others. She says, "I have new appreciation that every act and intention combines with those of others to affect the Universe. This wide compassionate circle has enlivened my own humanity."

For both Carlene and Clifford, a new awakening invited them to experience their humanity and become alive in accordance with the degree of their compassion. Ubuntu revealed to Clifford that being present to who he is in the context of others was an invitation to move beyond the enclosure of how he had perceived his value as a person. In the process, he realized, "I am discovering new layers of life about who I am." For Carlene, the enclosure of being physically distant from others revealed an opportunity to proactively engage in a wider circle of compassionate community through technology and social media.

How will your compassionate responses of showing up for life reveal that your humanity becomes alive to the degree of your compassion?

Stepping Across Lines

In the 1990s, I was a finalist in several search processes to lead high-profile congregations. In each case, when I was not selected, I was told, "We so wanted to hire you. If only you had not spoken about being gay and having a partner." Hearing those words was disappointing—and bittersweet. Beyond the bittersweet lay a profound, transformative truth. My intentional choice to step across the line of fear and enclosure, and be open about my sexuality in the context of my faith and my profession, represented a defining point in my journey. I had always believed that the image of the Holy is found in every person. Choosing the courage to be present to the presence of the Holy in me unfolded the layers of my own life to a deeper level of integrity, and a truer reflection of that presence in me.

In your relationships, you can choose freedom from enclosed living by being attentive to the subtle, emergent demarcating lines. Tracy and Sue had been in a spousal tug of war. They were each convinced that they were right about an issue they had argued over. Steadfast in their self-righteousness, skirmishes kept flaring up in their daily lives in the week that followed.

Tracy received an unexpected insight while out playing with their dog. He said, "I was so immersed in her joy in being out for a walk and the playfulness of playing fetch. I thought to myself, 'Sue and I are in danger of losing that kind of joy and playful spirit. For what purpose? Do I really need to be correct about some pissy argument?'"

He could have chosen to remain steadfast in his imagined correctness. Instead he saw an invitation in their dog's joyful playfulness. Tracy chose to reclaim what he most treasured about the relationship with Sue. That evening he said to Sue, "I'm sorry. Sorry for being so pig-headed." Sue was surprised and thankful. They both acknowledged that in that moment they could feel the tensions thaw. The positions they each staked out began to seem inconsequential compared to the freedom of emerging from behind a self-demarcated line.

The hard line began to dissipate as if being offered into the waters of the Universe for cleansing. Sue and Tracy discovered that a simple, heartfelt "I'm sorry" opens up sacred landscapes in a relationship where they were able to meet in the safe space it created. Instead of being closed off by ever-hardening positions, the field of their life opened up to becoming authentically human with one another.

Being correct is not a path that necessarily brings you more fully alive. Being aware of subtle lines within your relationships invites you to courageously step into proactive openness rather than withdraw into a life-sapping enclosure. Responding from your heart space with a seemingly simple "I'm sorry" opens a new landscape on which a relationship can flourish.

Your journey is defined by your response to the constant, ever-shifting fusion of elements in your life and being present to your evolving self. When you choose to internalize the distorted or limiting perceptions of others, it is natural to enclose yourself by drawing lines around what you can or can't do, who you can or can't be, or how you choose to reveal who you are to others. By the same token, your choices can empower you to become progressively more grounded in the reality of who you are.

As you choose to step across lines, you receive courage to show up in the context of others and to become present to the beauty in you that is a gift to the world.

Stepping Stone Three:
The Way of Compassion

One of the central tenets of the Celtic tradition is that what is deepest and most significant in us is the sacredness of the Holy One's image. One cherished image of the faith is of John, Jesus's beloved follower, leaning up against Jesus's chest—as if listening to the heartbeat of Love itself. What a magnificent invitation to be present to the heartbeat of that sacred image discovered in ourselves when we cross over our own lines of enclosure. It is a reminder to express deep tenderness toward ourselves when others tell us "If only you were...."

Tenderness toward your own self as you break out of enclosures, claim your voice, and learn to be present is experienced through cultivating the empathy that allows you to be compassionate. Your own journey leads to transformation as you befriend the texture of your life and experience your personal story through the lens of compassion. The way of compassion is crucial, because it transforms how you experience yourself, others, and the world.

Are You Good Enough?

Many of us carry a self-image with deep roots in our past reinforcing a perception that we are not quite "good enough." They are slights and hurts that you inflict upon yourself. The Holy One has no interest in you nursing images of not being good enough or unworthy of compassion. When you befriend—and therefore diminish—the negative energy of such self-perception, you cease being a victim who is controlled by the power of what you may dislike when you look in the mirror of your life.

In the Hebrew Scripture, mercy is always an expression of the Holy One's tenderness and compassion. As you develop empathy and mercy toward yourself, you begin to discover the luminous freeing presence of the merciful, compassionate Holy One in your life, so that you can radiate these same qualities in the world around you. This characteristic is infinitely more important than adherence to a legalistic way of life. In fact, mercy is so important that scripture reveals that even God is changed and left different as a result of the exercise of mercy. The Holy One even experiences empathy for humans who are merciful to themselves and others.

Mercy, love, and compassion are enlivening companions on your journey to a new way of being human. Of these three, love is at the core of your life, bringing you alive. By the same token, not loving yourself keeps you walled off from the love that is at the heart of the Universe and the Holy. Warren was aware enough to be transformed by this insight when he spent time in recovery for alcoholism in his forties.

Warren learned that having a Higher Power and telling the truth about himself were critical steps to recovery. The Holy was his Higher Power. Yet he lived with fear that speaking the truth about being gay would result in the Holy despising, even hating him. The religious messages he had received and internalized as a child told him that. While out walking the grounds of the treatment center one evening, Warren heard a voice say to him, "I told you to love one another. I didn't say what sex." In that moment Warren's life was shaken up. He said, "This was larger than I could see the edges of. Love is so much larger than I'd ever allowed myself to imagine."

Warren faced a choice to continue living within the enclosures of what he thought love meant, or to listen to the truth he'd heard and trust it enough to try it on.

Like Warren, daily meditations such as slowly repeating a phrase such as, "Come, Love; Come" or "Love" as you listen to your breath and body allows you to be attentive to the love that believes you are good enough. The old messages in the inbox of your brain begin to fade away as you immerse your life in this new truth. It becomes possible to admit the in-grained assumptions of not being good enough and to release their power. As these old messages fade, begin to practice a daily thankfulness for one thing that makes you lovable and good enough.

For Warren, this has resulted in living on a more fulsome landscape of his life that includes open, honest, loving relationships free of his old enclosures. In the transformation that ensues, you discover love and being good enough that is much more expansive than you had ever imagined.

In my late 30s, my spiritual guide asked me to do a daily exercise at home in front of a mirror. Each day I was to stand in front of the mirror looking into my own eyes and slowly name good, creative, loving, playful, strong, tender, magnificent, and courageous things about myself. My first reaction was to ask if this was an exercise in triteness. Then, I experienced an initial flood of memories of being 12 years old and not liking to look at myself in a mirror. As a result of being teased for being chubby, I'd imagined that I was fat. The mirror reminded me of how I had loathed looking at my young face. As adolescent memories continued to resurface alongside who I was as an adult, the real intent of the exercise became apparent. It was to create empathy and mercy with the layers of my personal journey and so develop a deeper compassion toward my own self. I was connecting with compassionate delight about who I am, and being present to myself.

This new, richly textured compassion revealed to me that I can never know the exact experiences of another person—whether it be a friend, colleague, or someone in a rural village in the Amazon—because I have not walked in their shoes. I said to my spiritual guide, "The mirror exercise has created a new attentiveness that I am good enough, and I'm discovering that empathy toward myself is opening up an enclosure. I'm realizing that my self-compassion allows me to imagine walking in the shoes of another. A spirituality of compassion is inviting me both deep within myself and connecting me with others in a merciful way."

Tilting, Turning, and Opening Your Heart

Every day you make choices to either assist in the birthing of who you are, or to craft a limiting container for yourself. As you trust your voice and become present to yourself, you will develop new appreciation for your place in the Universe. It may mean naming the struggles you have in believing that you are worthy of love. Or it may mean being gentle and compassionate to yourself for not being as empathetic as you would like to be. This frees you to offer compassion to your enemy as well.

Compassion is not an invitation to be a punching bag for others—there is nothing self-diminishing about the way of compassion. There is also nothing empowering about engaging the negative energy of hate. Choosing to hate—regardless of the reason—is a refusal to leave an enclosure. Compassion is the way out. Although you may not have the capacity to love the person you hate, you can express compassion by wanting what is best for them. Compassion will then free you to detach yourself from your need to hate. As we cultivate these practices of compassion, we tilt, turn, and open our hearts.

Many people embrace the Christian observance of Christmas—even those who profess no faith at all. The celebration of a vulnerable child evokes a universal empathy and hope transcending any one tradition, inviting an earthy re-connection with the compassion for which we are each hard-wired. Something about the image compels us to shift gears, and open our hearts. Through the years I have worked with people to become present to self-compassion by imagining the Christ child giggling away in his crib.

Sonja spoke with me about her personal struggle and desire to cross an enclosing line in her life. She told me, "I've played with your image of the Christ giggling away and it's opened up a new tenderness in me toward myself and the steps I need to take. It's impossible to be hard-hearted or closed off to a giggling child. I want to be that gentle with myself so that I can laugh with tender thankfulness about being compassionate to me. As I imagine this giggling one, I discover that my own heart turns, tilts, and opens to the Holy and to life, readying me to cross over the enclosure."

Tilting, turning, and opening your heart can be startling when it collides with assumptions about others that you have accepted as a given. On one of several peace missions to Israel and Palestine with groups of Jews and Christians, I was startled by an encounter reminding me of how simple words and being present can open an enclosure.

During the trip, we heard real, palpable fear from Israelis about security and suicide bombers. Many Israelis expressed a yearning to hear apologies from Palestinians. We heard stories from Palestinian women held at checkpoints and forced to give birth there because they were not allowed through. Many Palestinians yearned to hear apologies from Israelis. We met with those on both sides who had given their lives to bridging the divide and bringing both groups together.

We stood beneath the 28-foot-tall wall of concrete that was being built around Jerusalem. Palestinians viewed it as the building of an enclosure preventing hundreds of thousands from getting to their jobs or receiving medical treatment. Many Israelis said it was necessary for security and stopping the carnage of suicide bombers. Standing at the wall, we were all impacted by its declaration of muscular power.

Returning to the bus our group was largely silent, reflecting on what we'd seen, when suddenly a young Palestinian banged on the closed door of the bus and came rushing in. He was the driver for a French television crew that had been filming during our visit. He'd overhead an American Jew in our group respond to a spontaneous interview from the French reporter by saying he was ashamed of what he'd seen. The young Palestinian announced to our group, "I've never heard such a thing said. I love you. God bless you. God bless you. God bless you." And then he was gone.

By being present at the wall and verbalizing a heartfelt response to what he'd seen, one of our group had unexpectedly opened and tilted the heart of a young man who yearned to be acknowledged and seen as a human being. In return we received a lavish blessing from the Universe as he kept repeating "God bless you." Simple words of regret open up new heart spaces of surprising connection.

Likewise, your voice, words, actions, and compassion are part of your spiritual positioning system that creates space for the tilting, turning, and opening of hearts in everyday encounters. In the process, it shifts your experience of a new way of being human with others as you become part of reshaping the human story.

Laughter on the Journey to Your Center

Sonja wanted to return to the practice of walking a labyrinth to ground her in clarity and courage as she took the next steps in her life. This ancient practice is very different from walking a maze. When you enter a maze you are unable to see the way out. When you step into a labyrinth you see the entire labyrinth on the floor inviting you to walk the circuitous route to the center. Sonja experienced the practice of walking the labyrinth as going deeper and deeper into the heart of herself and the Holy to discover love and compassion. She knew that she could linger in the center, and when ready, follow the path back out.

Several weeks later, Sonja told me that a young girl joined her as she entered the labyrinth. "Look at all these people, walking like this," said the girl, as she mimicked the people slowly and intently walking the path. "We don't walk like that, we walk like this!" she said, grabbing Sonja's hand while skipping inside and outside the lines along their way to the labyrinth's center. As they continued, the girl laughed along the journey until interrupted by a man who disapprovingly said, "I don't think you're supposed to laugh while you do this." The girl's eyes grew wide as she kindly said to him, "I just can't help myself!"

As Sonja recounted the story she said, "This child was a surprising gift! I thought I had to follow the path as it is laid out but she taught me it's all right to cross over the lines. I used to think that walking the labyrinth had to be contemplative and serious, but we smiled and laughed on the journey to the center! She helped me see that I can be filled with laughter and compassion as I free myself from my enclosure."

When you live removed from laughter, it is a wakeup call that your grounding needs recalibrating. It is time to be open to the unexpected taps on your shoulder that invite you to pay attention to what laughter means along the path to a new way of being human.

Mitch was reflecting on an unexpected tap on his shoulder while attending a conference with a colleague of his. He said, "His infectious laughter reminded me that I'd stopped laughing very much." Mitch's initial reaction was to recoil from what this might mean for his own life. Instead of ignoring this tap on the shoulder, he embraced it as a gift and invitation to pay attention to.

His colleague's deep-within-the-belly laughter caused Mitch to ask why such laughter had become a rarity in his life. He mindfully offered this question on his daily meditative walks. It became clear to Mitch that his inability to forgive himself for whatever part he played in a broken relationship was choking his laughter.

Mitch began the work of forgiving and being compassionate to himself. In the process, Mitch became appreciative of the connective tissue between his emotions, body, and thoughts. As his laughter returned, Mitch understood that the oneness of his own life was being repaired. The restoration of laughter became a metaphor for Mitch of the journey to the center of what ails and enlivens the journey to being fully alive.

With tenderness and the laughter of taking ourselves lightly, the way of compassion invites us into richly textured living and discovering a new way to be human. Compassion releases us from the confinement of believing that our lives are about ourselves. We may each only be able to save the life we are responsible for, but the mercy and empathy inherent in compassion create a bond that links us to the DNA of the Universe and the Holy. The result is that we become awake to our oneness with others no matter which part of the planet they are on.

Reflect:

- What will you do today to be awake to the Holy discovered in your voice or that of another person? How will it change your relationship with yourself, the Holy, and others?

- How will you be present to yourself today? Can you imagine how this will be a gift to the world?

- What choice will you make today to be compassionate? What positive energy will this unleash?

Spirited Practices

- Give thanks daily for one experience of trusting how you have used or celebrated your voice that day.

- Create one or two Being Present moments every day. They might be five or 10 minutes when you sit in a quiet space concentrating on listening to the flow of your breath through your body.

- Begin each day with an intention. Invite compassion into your day—self-compassion and compassion for those you will engage with this day.

Follow your bliss for your soul's high adventure.
—Joseph Campbell

Pathway Three:
Risky Invitations

"Biko's death cannot go unanswered," I said. "None of us want to sit back and be passive, do we?" asked Maureen as she looked around the room where seven of us sat cradling mugs of tea. We all shook our heads in silent agreement. I said, "It's why we're here. I feel helpless and I want to do something." We were beginning to respond to a risky invitation. I had no idea that the journey we were about to embark on would reveal so much about being spiritually and physically present.

Steve Biko was a hero to many of us. He was widely regarded as the most significant black leader to have emerged in South Africa since Nelson Mandela's imprisonment. In 1977, while being held in custody, he was killed by the authorities. In an attempt to crush the reactions to his death, all public gatherings of more than three people had been declared to be illegal. The organizations he founded were among many that were summarily shut down by the government.

In his death I realized that the government's desire to control, to dehumanize, and deny happiness to others was like a voracious demon with an insatiable appetite. As we sat with Maureen's question, one person said, "We can begin by praying." I suggested, "What if our prayers become part of an eight-day fast leading up to Biko's funeral?" The willingness to give something up in order to be awake to new possibilities stood in contrast to the lust to deny the humanity of others that would stop at nothing to achieve its goal.

Our small group of university students and faculty members began to shape a fast that would include meeting for daily prayer, meditation, discussion, and support. None of us had ever imagined being part of something like this. The chapel at Rhodes University would remain open around the clock for anyone who wanted to pray for the country.

Even as we planned a fast built around prayer, meditation, and discussion, our raw emotions ranged from anger and disbelief to mourning and lamentation. "What if we took some visible action?" I then quickly added, "As much as praying, let's engage people in thinking about what is happening in our country."

"But what about the ban on public gatherings of more than three people?" someone asked. I felt fear at the mention of this ban, because I knew that contravention of it would result in harsh actions from the authorities for whom human lives were dispensable. I said, "Let's think about a procession of mourners in which you only see one mourner at a time." The idea electrified the group. Quickly we decided that the university's tradition of wearing black academic gowns in the dining halls at night could become the dress code of a planned procession whose route would be through the main street of the college town. One person at a time would travel the route wearing a black gown, carrying a wreath in their hands. So our protest march of mourning and lamentation was born as a companion to the fast.

Two days later, the phone rang in my dorm. "Please withdraw from this fast and protest," my parents demanded. They had seen the photograph of me in the protest march that had appeared in several South African newspapers. "We're scared for your safety. You know what happens to people who speak up in this country."

Only months before, I had come out to my family as a gay man, and our conversation reflected the strained but cordial communication that existed between us. As they implored me to "be quiet," I said, "What if people had spoken out against the Nazis? What if we worked for the humanity of every person instead of rejecting, excluding, or killing?" Our conversation ended tersely.

I woke up in the early hours of the morning, thinking about the conversation with my parents. I wanted to talk to others about whether our prayers, protest, and fasting were enough of a response. At 7 a.m., I was in the chapel for our morning meditation time. I finally interrupted the silence and said, "Let's attend Biko's funeral." No sooner had I uttered the word than I thought, "You must be crazy Robert!" Was this a wildly risky thing to suggest—or was I trusting my intuition and imagination? Or both?

I was discovering that meditation, prayer, and fasting were not solitary acts of spirituality. I found them inviting a response. It seemed inconceivable to not be physically present when we had become so spiritually present to that moment in time.

My parents upon learning of our plans, said, "We implore you not to attend. They're predicting violence and rioting. We want you to be safe."

"Mom and Dad," I responded, "Going to the funeral is like saying that love is stronger than death. I have to show up—for me."

On the day of the funeral, we left early on a bus that would drive us several hundred miles to the football stadium in which it would be held. Our small band of college students quickly noticed the helicopters flying overhead and the talk about police informers photographing those present. We entered a stadium filled with more than 30,000 people.

At the end of a daylong African funeral, a very short man appeared on the stadium field. He told the crowds, "God loves you. Please be God's partners in love. If you take up violence you will become just like those who have killed Biko." He begged the mourning crowd to find another way to end apartheid. "With violence, you will lose your humanity," he said. This man of small stature with a towering message was Desmond Tutu; he and Nelson Mandela were the two men most vilified by the government. He had the crowd in the palm of his hand. Every person was straining forward so as not to miss a single word or inflection.

Back at the campus, a South African curry with its intriguing blend of spices, vegetables, and meat that had simmered for hours, seemed to be a fitting meal for the breaking of our fast. Over the meal, we spoke about Tutu's invitation that continued to reverberate in our conversation. One person said, "He treated everyone like an adult with a choice to make about where our hearts belong."

In responding to being both physically and spiritually present in this time of turmoil, I began to understand the pathway of responding to risky invitations.

What are risky invitations? Risky invitations interrupt the imagined or assumed course of your life, raising the stakes right where you struggle the most. Responding to these invitations takes you beyond your comfort zone, inviting transformation and an enlarged understanding of yourself, others, and the Holy. The perceived risk compared to what you imagine to be certain may tempt you to decline the invitation. Don't say no just yet!

When you clutch at the imagined certainties of your life, you keep life at bay, and drain and distance yourself from your journey with the Holy. To turn back from the risky invitations of your journey is to trifle with life by willfully denying yourself the fullness of who you are meant to be.

As you cease to clutch at what you know, you will come to appreciate your journey with new tenderness. Living with unclenched hands frees you to be partners with the Holy. The risky invitations are much more than a surprise disrupting your familiar patterns; they are a gift connecting you with others in new mindfulness about what it means to be fully human. In accepting risky invitations, your transformation switches on a light by which you see the journey ahead with new eyes.

Our lives are replete with refusals and acceptances. It is never too late on your journey to develop mindful openness to the risky invitations presented to you.

There are three stepping stones that allow us to be present to the risky yet life-giving invitations of our journey.

1. You are loved for your existence—loved for simply being.

2. Trusting and cultivating your imagination—you are part of the limitless imagination of the Holy.

3. Polishing the world—reflecting the imaginative love of the Holy.

These simple truths create a way of being that allows you to discern and accept the risky invitations presented to you along your journey.

Stepping Stone One: You Are Loved for Your Existence

Your existence is cause for thanksgiving. Yet many of us have internalized the unfortunate trinity of "would, should, and could." We've heard the direction "If only you could…" or, "You should…." We've even participated in keeping ourselves from our bliss with the excuse that "I would if…." It results in keeping us distant from the truth that we are loved because we exist. The Holy has no use for such self-diminishment.

Tender Words About You

When you live with the belief that something about you makes you weak or not good enough, it is difficult to enter into mutual relationships seeking the best for each person. When you do not see your own belovedness and magnificence, it's difficult to think about being a healthy person, much less imagining a mutual relationship with other people. There is disequilibrium within you and your relationships. The tenderness of the Holy yearns to be known in you.

I was haunted by Tutu's words at the Biko funeral: "God loves you. Please be God's partners in love." I felt enlivened by what this truth meant for others. I was not able to believe that it could also be true for me. It felt like a chasm that could not be breached, leaving an aching presence inside of me. At the time, I felt unable and unsafe to give voice to the turmoil this caused for me.

My immediate family and close friends knew that I was gay. The year before attending Biko's funeral, I had been accepted as a candidate for ordination to the priesthood in the Anglican Church by the man who had prayed with me for healing, Archbishop Bill Burnett. His prayers had changed my life, and I was grateful, yet I knew that he was vehemently opposed to ordaining anyone who was gay.

As I wrestled with my desire to live a life of integrity, I knew that the work I felt called to as a priest would not be possible if I revealed my sexuality to him. In fact, Bill Burnett had been known to send people for treatments to "cure" them of their homosexuality. As a result of this, the seminary located in the town where I was a university student had an underground, closeted group of gay seminarians living in fear of being discovered.

Where did Tutu's passionate proclamation of being loved by a God who invited us to be partners with the Holy connect with Archbishop Burnett's message that one part of a person's life excluded him or her from such love? I continued to pray each day to be healed of my sexuality.

Months later, my spiritual advisor said some simple words to me in response to this internal struggle of mine. "God loves you for your existence," he said. It was an even more seismic truth than Tutu's assurance of God's love. I was struck by the firm clarity of his declaration and the tenderness of his words. This was a truly risky invitation to move beyond the fears of loving the fullness of who I am and into the luminous generosity of the Holy. I was beginning to discover that the spaciousness and generosity of love is the single lens by which spirituality and our own lives should be approached.

Goodness and Bliss in You

Many of us grew up without ever hearing simple, tender words like the ones spoken to me by my spiritual advisor. They point to a way of relationship and life that is enlivening. Part of our experience is being valued for what we produce or do, what we can do for another, how useful we appear to be, or even what we can get from one another. In becoming fully alive, to be loved for your existence, shifts the ground of how you engage with life while discovering goodness and bliss on your journey.

The invitation I heard in Tutu's words and those of my spiritual advisor revealed a stepping stone to the truth. Spiritual wisdom is discovered in knowing that we are each made for goodness and bliss as much as we are made to love and be loved. Discovering your bliss and goodness is the testing ground of being loved for your existence. My test came via the internalized homophobia I experienced on my life journey. People of color and women often experience internalized racism or sexism. Although you cannot control the fears or reactions of others, you can avoid subtly appropriating the toxic negativity or blindness of those who cannot see you in your fullness. Anchoring to your goodness will remind you of who you are and defuse the potential impact of those who attempt to assault or infect who you are.

One day, as my friend Laura and I discussed a community initiative on ending homelessness, she unexpectedly asked me, "Do you think I'm a good person? So many people assume I'm bad because I've been homeless. But I don't think I'm bad." I felt torn apart by her words. Laura had once become homeless as a result of domestic violence, and yet she steadfastly refused to speak of herself as a victim because she believed that victimhood could all too easily define her personhood. I had admired her tireless advocacy on behalf of the homeless for many years. Her perspective had challenged the perspectives and changed the hearts and minds of so many people, and yet here she was, questioning her own goodness. I felt protective of Laura, yet knew that only she could befriend and therefore let go of the insidious comments about her worth as a person.

Later that day, I attended a lavish reception honoring a public celebrity when a man named Lars pulled me aside and said, "I need to chat with you." In the comfort of a quiet space, Lars hesitantly said, "I've never had the courage to ask you this before, but I need to know if you think I'm a good person. I really want to be a good person." My heart ached for Lars. I'd first encountered him as a mentor of young men and women who were starting out in the high-tech world and eager for healthy models of leadership. His generosity in creating and teaching compassion went beyond financial giving and technological resources to include his own active personal involvement.

As we spoke that evening, Lars said he felt judged by some for his financial resources and that the assumption often made was that as a person of wealth he was somehow tainted or "bad." Only Lars could befriend the fullness of who he is and detach from the negative energy that was clouding his goodness and bliss.

Laura and Lars each knew a profound, life-giving bliss in their respective work of polishing the world. The authenticity of their goodness was unsettling to some, threatening to shroud their work and curtail their energy. Each had responded to a risky invitation to follow their bliss and reframe the human story by inviting compassion toward others. Their challenge now was to choose to decline the invitation to see themselves as "bad" and instead place their life energy within the spirit of goodness and bliss.

Your bliss is measured by those activities that bring you deeply alive. Like a flickering lighthouse lamp helping me to navigate my way to the truth that I am loved for my existence, the bliss of the activities I was engaged in on the path to ordination was enlivening to me. I could not let go of the hopeful truth that I was worthy of such bliss—even with competing voices declaring that I was not fully acceptable because of part of who I was.

I poured over the Biblical stories of the women and men that flocked to Jesus. Most of them were not loved or fully accepted for their existence. In every instance, they left the encounter with him changed or transformed by the luminous love that he showed them. With each reading of the stories, I became more aware of the extraordinary mutuality present in this rabbi's encounters with those who had the courage to discover becoming more fully alive. In some of the stories, you feel the fear with which people leave his presence. Not a fear of him, but a fearful fleeing or turning back from a moment of truth about being loved for their existence. He sparked in them a discovery of their goodness, pointing to their bliss in becoming fully alive.

Like them, some of us fear allowing this unveiled truth to rest in the spacious container that is your life. When this happens, you are holding back from being willing to cohabitate with the truth being revealed. Instead, you are invited to test out the truth, explore it, and wrestle with it. That is where the moments of epiphany and transformation begin to emerge.

Beyond Conditional Love

Love is the grounding, framework, and lens through which everything is viewed. The pulse of the Holy and of the Universe is love. The risky invitation that I accepted at the time of Biko's death opened a pathway to an even more risky invitation to love myself. As partners in the work of love with the Holy, it is never a love for us alone. We are invited to be free of conditional love as we team up with others to seek happiness for all people.

As I cohabitated with this truth about myself, I gleaned from my Buddhist friends their teaching about love as the desire for others to be happy. Reflecting Christ's teaching of loving yourself as much as the Holy or other people, it went further. It offered new insight into love being expressed through working for the well-being of others. This Buddhist insight startled me because it came with no strings or conditions attached to love.

My own experience of loving myself conditionally and transposing that perspective onto the Holy began to shift. I gleaned from Buddhist practice that the "near enemy" of love is conditional love. Through the decades in my work with others, I've discovered that many grow up with and carry into their adult lives the internalized message that love is given or withheld based on actions that others expect to see in us. Conditional love is not love. It might be a contractual or transactional relationship, but it is not love.

Brian and I became friends after being seat companions on a six-hour flight across the United States. As we talked about building loving relationships as the purpose of life, Brian spoke about how he tried to live his life by connecting with people at a spiritual level. He said, "I always try to connect with the core of another person. I'm all about trust, because trust builds love and love allows you to honor one another's core; when that happens, I've discovered that we can count on one another." Acknowledging that trust takes work and time, along with a willingness to go beyond your comfort zone with another person, Brian spoke about how this has changed his personal and business relationships, "When this happens you live with relationships that are unconditional, knowing that each of you is doing the best that you can with what you have."

As our conversation progressed, it was clear that his five years of marriage to Marika had shaped his path of building loving relationships. Brian's first marriage of 25 years ended in divorce, in spite of years of counseling to try to reimagine and rebuild the marriage. Brian said, "I was startled by how my many religious friends cast me out. It was all black or white for them, and I was wrong in their eyes to have divorced. My adult children told me I was rationalizing my selfishness, and they avoided me as much as they could."

Conditional love from his religious friends and children was a chilling experience for Brian. He could have chosen to reject the path he embarked on and accept the invitation to be trapped. Instead, he chose to follow his emerging inner spiritual positioning system of building trusting, loving relationships on the new landscape of his life. "I wasn't divorcing my children or religious friends," he said. He expressed sorrow for their feelings and invited them to "Take time to hear what's going on in each other's lives and reactions. The anger will change." The result has been that time, apologies to one another for unintended sorrows, and a willingness to be present to each other in the unfolding emotional angst has given way to unconditional loving relationships with his children. His religious friends have remained enmeshed in their rectitude.

Brian and his children have each acknowledged that it was the promise of birthing unconditional, loving relationships that sustained each of them as they worked through their own issues within their capacity at the time. Brian observed that, "We can only be as good to others as we are to ourselves; we can only love others to the degree we love ourselves."

To live beyond conditional love invites awareness from you of the life-sapping energy of conditional living. You are not a conditional human being because life and the Universe long for your unconditional love in order to discover a new way of being human.

I often use the image of each person given an angel at birth. This angel walks in front of you saying, "Make way! Behold! Here comes the face of God!" The angel declares to the world that people should pay attention because you are approaching and you represent something of the Holy. This angel says that you have a place of privilege, goodness, beauty, and love. It is an angel egging us on, because we are loved for our existence. There is nothing conditional about this declaration.

When I first imagined this angel walking in front of me, I began to understand why Tutu's exhortation to "Please be God's partners in love" had terrified me. The angel invites each of us to take our place in the world as an unconditional companion and partner with the Holy. It is an encouraging angel, reminding us that we are loved for being.

Accepting risky invitations occurs in relationship to our intentions and how mindful we are about the precepts and values we choose to live by. We are changed by what we love. We are shaped by what we seek to love and where we put our life energy. Along the way, we become enlivened by the unexpected love received from others. Love is never about self-negation or the negation of another person. The result is that our hearts and lives are expanded in realizing that each person is loved for their existence—unconditionally.

In accepting a risky invitation, the journey reveals that your existence is cause for giving thanks!

Stepping Stone Two: Trusting and Cultivating Your Imagination

We each have the capacity to understand something without having it explained to us. We are capable of imagining ourselves in the shoes of others just as we can place ourselves in the mind of another. When we are mindful about the core spiritual and human values of love and compassion, our lives become oriented to being aware and awake to life around us. On this fertile soil, our intuition and imagination are engaged.

❖ ❖ ❖ ❖ ❖ ❖ ❖ ❖ ❖ ❖ ❖ ❖ ❖ ❖ ❖ ❖ ❖

Respond or Life Will Pass You By

Your responses to the risky invitations of life depend upon your own mindfulness. Cultivating mindfulness leads us into a new way of being human, because it connects us more fully with our own humanity, with the Holy, and with our own oneness with others.

The choice to remain within known enclosures and relate primarily with those who reaffirm the often cozy line we draw around life is a self-fulfilling, unimaginative place to live in, which we are unlikely to be curious about being in the shoes of another. The "other"—perhaps an Ethiopian cab driver and his family, a person of a different sexual orientation, someone whose attire identifies them belonging to an unfamiliar spiritual tradition, homeless teenagers on the street—may then become a source of anxiety, or someone to be dismissed or feared. In such a way of life, imagination is not exercised, effectively freeze-drying your humanity like the prepared meals used by hikers and campers. The good news is that like those dehydrated meals that come to life when mixed with water, your imagination and intuition never die. However, they do need to be cultivated and trusted in awakening to the journey of becoming fully alive.

Where did my idea for an eight-day fast, followed by a procession of mourners, come from? I believe my response flowed intuitively from my mindfulness of the precepts of my life. It was an early introduction to the practice of trusting and cultivating my imagination. It was a moment to respond and engage with the invitation, or let it pass me by.

My life was transformed in accepting the risky invitation that Biko's murder presented. I had not set out to engage in a fast, much less to lead one. I never expected to lead a procession of people protesting an appalling event. I was unprepared for the invitation that presented itself to be spiritually and physically present at the funeral. Each could have been viewed as a separate risky invitation, disturbing my expectations and comfort zone. Together, they were an invitation with implications for how I would respond to being fully alive.

Your fear of speaking up in response to life can leave your life embalmed like a withering corpse. By contrast, when you live with the truth that it is more difficult to remain silent than to speak, you refuse to let life pass you by. You know that the Universe itself longs for your response to life, and you allow yourself to become fully alive in the present.

My friend Chris is a peace activist who quickly became involved in a peace organization when she moved to a small city in the Eastern United States. For years, she struggled with a member of the group who seemed to project her own shadows onto Chris as if longing to be Chris. The bright ideas and energy that Chris brought to the group were constantly thwarted by this other person.

Chris's lifetime of work in the area of reconciliation fed her desire to reconcile and find a way to work together with her nemesis. After four years of attempting to reconcile and work together, Chris realized that intervention from a professional mediator would be helpful. Following the intervention the tension and discomfort eased—only to reappear with vengence about 18 months later. Chris observed that, "The peace and reconciling work of the organization was being held back because of how this woman's projections of me seemed so present in every organizing meeting. I felt like I was allowing life to pass me by because of this constant distraction. It seemed so at odds with the work we were committed to. One day it became clear that I needed to detach by getting out of her neighborhood."

As she worked through this revelation, Chris was invited to participate in a conversation about the formation of a new peace group to be housed by an inclusive religious community who wanted to use a chapel on their property for vigils and prayers that would ground the work of peacemaking and reconciliation. It was a risky invitation for Chris because of her steadfast belief that reconciliation is always possible. If she continued to clutch onto that hope for repairing a broken relationship, she would let life pass her by and so diminish her voice, joy, and gifts.

She spoke up by accepting the invitation to become part of the new peace organization, and instead of letting life pass her by, she has embraced life, thereby allowing it to embrace her. The result has been a rekindling of her passion and bliss.

❧ ❧ ❧ ❧ ❧ ❧ ❧ ❧ ❧ ❧ ❧ ❧ ❧ ❧ ❧ ❧ ❧

Likewise, your risky invitation to speak up through your actions or voice is a choice presenting itself to you on the path to a new way of being human and becoming fully alive. With each affirmative response, you participate in offering hope and goodness within the human family and Creation. Trusting yourself to do so is enlivening and transformative.

Beyond Failure—How Life Can Be

The temptation in our times of personal failure or crisis is to return to the very things that have not worked and have led to the predicament in which we find ourselves. Imagination, however, invites us both into and beyond ourselves. It is like an upside-down map of the world in which you are surprised to see South and Central America, Africa, and Australia placed above North America, Asia, and Europe. The vast masses of land are still there, but the upside-down map invites us to look at them differently. Cultivating our imagination is never to deny who we are or what has formed us, but rather, to see ourselves—and others—with new eyes.

In accepting the risky invitation that life presented, my daily meditation during the eight-day fast included reading the text of the Song of Mary, also known as the Magnificat. Mary, believed by Christians to be the mother of Christ, is revered in Islam, among native peoples in Central and South America and those who identify as not being religious but spiritual. She sings a song while pregnant with the Christ. It is lyrical intuition and imagination at its finest. I always wonder what must have been in her mind as she sings about the child in her womb that will re-imagine human relationships. Her song is about a new way of being human and alive.

In the failures of my own life, Mary's song reminds and nudges me to move beyond whatever pain, disappointment, sadness, or regret I may experience in the moment. I've come to believe that Tutu's words at Biko's funeral were about imagination as much as they were about love. My own moments of failure are often a crisis of lack of imagination.

I've continued to return to the Magnificat over many decades, marveling at the courage, awareness, and intuitive imagination of this teenage mother. In accepting the risky invitations at the time of Biko's death, I was not consciously aware of the impact that this text had on me. Many Christians understand Mary to be co-creatrix with the Holy, reflecting the imagination of God. Mary reminds us that to be human is to imagine things being better than they are. The wisdom tradition of Mary's song of imagination offered grounding to accept the invitation presented to me rather than let life pass me by.

Limitless Imagination

Reflecting on the risky invitations to which I have responded, I've come to see that we are made in the image, and in the imagination, of the Holy. This truth places our own innate imagination in the context of endless imagination. We are participants in the Divine imagination of how things might be—in our own lives and in the world around us.

The closest word to human in Hebrew or to the Latin *homo* is Adam. As we explore the meaning of Adam, we discover that it derives from the Hebrew root word meaning "imagination." Adam is a metaphor in the Abrahamic traditions for each person and the free will each of us exercises to choose harmful or beneficial actions. Your humanity is like the Garden of Eden, inviting you to blossom and flourish. Your journey is replete with invitations to make choices about tending that garden and creating a world of well-being and happiness for all.

To be human is to be part of limitless imagination. It is a gift for how we each participate in sustaining, encouraging, and nourishing divinity in us. We have the capacity to impact and even grow the Holy. Not some of us, but each of us! Your imagination is necessary in order to nourish the divinity within you and essential to the well-being of the world. This is what Tutu's invitation meant about being a partner with the Holy in creating a more loving and just world: in cultivating and trusting your imagination, you participate in expanding divinity, and so shape the dreams of a loving and just God who invites you into limitless imagination.

Zelda discovered the transformative gift of limitless imagination when she connected her professional expertise with a personal passion that she had shut out of her life. Zelda's friends and colleagues have admired her work in corporate social responsibility and leading international development programs. I have also always admired the jewelry that Zelda wears and that she has acquired from local craft people around the world. Responding to my observation about her eye for unique and beautiful jewelry Zelda said, "In every piece I admire the vision of the artist; they are such divergent expressions of how beauty is understood and realized. They remind me of my oneness with others, and every time I look at the bracelet or ring I'm wearing I'm grounded in the fact that every aspect of my life's work is an expression of releasing beauty in the lives of others."

One day Zelda explained how she had made some of the jewelry she was wearing. I was intrigued to learn more about this side of her life and was surprised when she wistfully said, "I haven't made jewelry in years because I always seem to be too busy to make time for it." A few months later Zelda called to say, "I've thought a lot about our conversation; I realized I was making excuses and denying the invitation to let go of the pause button on my imagination."

Several months later we had lunch together and Zelda was eager to tell me of the new jewelry studio she had set up in her home. She said, "As Americans we love to focus on the end result and I'm very results oriented, but I have been learning new lessons about another way of life." Zelda spoke of the process of making jewelry from various metals, rediscovering that she was entering a process that required her to be fully present. She said, "Metal can be molded and formed and cutting it is like cutting butter; it invites my imagination to be engaged and responsive in the moment." As Zelda described the gift of her skills catching up with her ideas she reflected that to her surprise her jewelry making had become a spiritual practice saying, "My position and posture become critical; it is a very Zen experience each time for me."

In saying yes to the risky invitation to listen to her passion Zelda unexpectedly discovered new skills for her professional and personal life in being present instead of focusing only on end results. Her imagination was reengaged revealing to her that the beauty of a new way of being human is discovered in allowing limitless imagination to meet the supple metal that is formed and shaped in unexpected displays of imaginative splendor.

The risky invitations that life offers to each of us present us with choices to accept or decline them. It is in accepting them, often not knowing where exactly they will lead us, that our intuition and imagination cheers us on. As much as we are loved for our existence, we are enlivened as we allow imagination to be an active partner in saying yes!

Stepping Stone Three: Polishing the World

Grounded in being loved for your existence, and steeped in limitless imagination, you discover that your journey invites you to polish the world. It is easy to be disheartened by how much polishing the world needs and to discard your gifts by asking what difference you make in putting them to use. Don't give up! When you walk away from polishing the world you curve inward with an ever-cramped and confining view of being human. Conversely, accepting that others need your unique gifts causes you to curve outward with unclenched hands. Ask yourself how your hands can polish the world. The resulting invitation may surprise you!

Relatives of the Holy

In accepting the risky invitations presented to me by the fast and participation in Biko's funeral, I received a gift. As I looked around me at the people in the packed football stadium, I was aware of being a minority. Surveying the crowd during the course of the day, I realized that this did not matter, because we are each a minority in some setting. Being together that day, our presence spoke to our oneness. I began to consciously ask what it means for each of us to be a relative of the Holy. It was a transformative moment.

It was an epiphany to think of the Holy as being lonely and wanting to create family. In the intervening years, my meditation and spirit practices have been enriched in imagining a God who yearns for touch and who wants to share tears, laughter, and hope with others. Imagine—the Holy wanting to stroll, walk, or hike with us along the journey through life!

Your experience of difference or being a minority in certain circumstances can lead you to turn inward. It then becomes easy to curve in on your own self, becoming defensive about your life and your place in the world. The journey to becoming fully human invites us to turn outward, experiencing and welcoming our connection with others. It is in the delight of being a relative of the rest of humanity that our desire for the happiness of others and our intuitive imagination meet, revealing that we can each polish the world. Every kindness and small action joins with those performed by others in loving the world.

In that football stadium, I discovered that I was part of a human family who would not allow hope to be imprisoned. Hope is an orientation that looks beyond the present at what might be, and works to achieve it. Hope affirms the life and dignity of each person. I learned that those who try to control us—and our imagination—attempt to separate us from the dream of God that each of our relatives in the human family will know happiness.

On that day at Biko's funeral, the show of police and military force was intended to squelch the hope and imagination of ending apartheid. Yet millions of gestures and actions around the world affirming the humanity and sacredness of every person in that country seemed to build instead—one upon the other. Each action declared hope in polishing the world. The relatives of the Holy seeking justice, mercy, and kindness, and the unstoppable hope of ordinary people ultimately overwhelmed the forces intent on denying the well-being of each relative.

Every conversation, each action that you take matters. Nothing is wasted.

What if those who imagined the ending of slavery, the right of women to vote, civil rights in the United States, or the early environmental movement had turned their backs on imagination and hope? What if they had succumbed to the prevailing wisdom that polishing the world was doomed to failure? Like them, our willing participation in hope is part of birthing something new for ourselves and our relatives in the human family. We polish not because of a guaranteed outcome or certainty of success, but because imaginative love for others will not, and cannot, be enclosed.

I have participated in the annual observance of Holocaust Memorial Day, and witnessed the reading of the names of those killed in the Holocaust. It is a chilling experience. Those who attend come from a wide variety of faith traditions, choosing to show up and embrace the precept of affirming life, regardless of their differences. This event—Unto Every Person There Is A Name—is a stark reminder that every relative in the human family has a name and a story that is sacred ground.

Your presence at such gatherings, whether it be about the Holocaust, protecting the rainforests, supporting the freedom of Tibetans, or speaking out against sexual abuse, is in every case a declaration of hope. Your presence is an intentional consciousness reflecting the orientation of your heart. You are declaring that you will not be a bystander or interloper in the fabric of life—you will show up to polish the world.

Where Does Your Heart Belong?

Your heart is enlarged, changed, and renewed as you connect with your relatives in the human family. My friend Peggy discovered this truth as she visited those affected by HIV/AIDS in Africa. It is the women of Guguletu, a suburb outside of Cape Town, whom she has carried in her heart since the trip. These young mothers discovered their own HIV status when they were tested for the virus following the deaths of their young children. Instead of being maudlin or resigned to their fate, Peggy experienced a spirit of aliveness forged through the shared grief of these mothers who had created a cooperative bead-making venture. There was a oneness of spirit about these women who believe that the beaded AIDS badges they produce will prevent other mothers from becoming infected and losing their children.

None of us would seek the risky invitation that was extended through grief to these women. The women of Guguletu reminded Peggy that for each of us the journey to becoming fully alive invites us deeper into the losses, truths, and ambiguities of life. Peggy left with a reverential respect for the way in which their risky invitation led them to polish the world.

In the sprawling suburb of Kayelitsha, a vast and ever-expanding area filled with flimsy shacks for as far as the eye can see, most people survive on meager incomes. At an AIDS orphanage in Kayelitsha, Peggy noticed that each room bore a sign that declared "Any Child is My Child." In the midst of crushing poverty, the sign was a reminder that we are one another's relatives and that the care of these orphans was an affirmation of polishing the world. Peggy reflected on what she had experienced, saying, "I learned that nobody can do everything, but everybody can do something. My heart was burst open by the generosity of love in action from people who have so little materially but whose hearts are offered to one another."

But what if you are ambiguous or despondent about the invitation to engage with and polish the world? Instead of living within the cloud of disengagement, there is an invitation presenting itself to you.

My friend Joe says, "I used to loathe the news and its negativity, because it made me feel helpless every day. I was determined to stop reading or listening to it." Joe received an unexpected risky invitation from a colleague who said, "In those stories there is an invitation directed to you for you to make a difference; why don't you become a partner with the Universe in making the world a little better, kinder, and more just?"

Joe could have chosen to ignore the invitation, but instead he chose to explore it. Paying new attention to the news, Joe realized that he was repeatedly drawn to stories about girls not having access to education in many parts of the world. He set out to learn more, devouring information and discovering ordinary people working in partnership with others to create schools and educational programs, along with those working to change cultural and religious perspectives that demeaned or limited the humanity of girls. Joe's previous sense of despondent helplessness was transformed into being enlivened by what was being revealed to him.

The result is that Joe volunteers his time with others to help build schools in partnership with local communities in Southeast Asia. He says, "I am so alive because of this work that I find myself always talking to others about the need to access education for girls." Then he added, "The risky invitation I received transformed my life! I needed to open my eyes and be willing to shift my consciousness."

In place of his old solitary cynicism about the news, Joe has learned a new truth on the path to a new way of being human. His contributions may be small when measured against the magnitude and scope of the need for girls education, but in working with others the collective power of hope, change, and shifting consciousness reminds him that in union with others our smallest of actions flow into the river of becoming fully human, fully alive.

As a result, Joe's own spirituality has shifted because of his work. He says, "I experience every day that I am part of an amazing human family, because we are all related to one another as much as we are relatives of the Holy. I learn from others in local communities a continent away as much as I do from those I work with at home on this issue."

Your life prepares you to respond to a risky invitation that brings you fully alive and that the Universe will be deprived of unless you choose to respond. When my uncle died alone in a nursing home in Africa, isolated from everyone, many family members expressed their sadness about his angry and lonely life. For decades, family members had recoiled from Colin's disdain for others and his inappropriate behavior.

It would have been easy to feel sadness and pity only for the choices Colin had made in his life. A fuller picture of his life included the one thing that I remembered bringing him alive and causing him to shine.

His passion was ignited by his love of an unspoiled mountainside and beach called Sandy Bay, a few miles from the city center of Cape Town. Beloved by naturalists and nature lovers, the pristine quality of Sandy Bay was threatened by plans to develop it for housing. The threat of development caused Colin to spring to life and become an unlikely leader of a movement to save Sandy Bay from development. His small band of disorganized preservationists persisted and were often apprehended, fined, and even thrown in prison overnight for their protests. But they succeeded and today it is a treasured, protected, and undeveloped place.

Colin could be found most weekends at Sandy Bay with a palpable joy about a corner of creation that had been preserved for others to delight in. If creation is also a relative of the Holy, then Colin has found a way to polish and protect the flora and fauna of that place.

I do not know if Colin resisted other risky invitations to shine and so be alive in his life. I do know that his life prepared him to respond to at least one risky invitation that made a difference. Likewise, you may choose to respond to only a few such invitations in your life, but with each response your place in the Universe with the relatives of the Holy shifts and deepens.

As you discover the truth that, with Creation and all of humanity, we are part of the relatives of the Holy, your place and purpose becomes engaged and enlivened as you help to create the narrative of a new way to be human. As you shine with this new truth, you invite others to do so as well.

Kindness Is Possible Every Day

It is tempting to think only about polishing the world in distant places or in response to egregious circumstances. Your everyday interactions with others invite a response just as significant. It is not a question of one kind of polishing versus another, or whether one is more important. Rather it is the daily opportunities of human contact that plead for us to be aware and awake to what the present moment invites of you.

Your kindness polishes the world in the course of your daily life. The Hebrew prophet Micah says there are three things that the Holy asks us to integrate into our lives: "To do justice, to love kindness, and to walk humbly with your God." To be just and to be humble are not enough by themselves. Micah suggests that our practice of kindness is as defining of our life as anything else.

Practicing kindness reflects how we wish to travel through life, placing great worth and value on each of the relatives of the Holy. When we place value on kindness, we accept it as a gift and it remains a gift—instead of becoming a possession—when we continually give it away. Polishing the world with kindness creates a gift economy of life. As you practice the gift economy, kindness accrues value as a significant new currency in circulation.

By example, I have never forgotten the conversation I had with a clerk in a grocery store. I was in line and he was ringing up my purchases. My intuition led me to ask, "So how are you dealing with your day?" As if waiting for someone to ask this question, he quickly told me about a sadness that he was dealing with in his life, adding that he knew he'd be all right, but that he'd felt off-balance and troubled all day. There were others in line behind me and the conversation lasted no more than a few minutes. As I picked up my bags, he said to me, "Thank you for being so kind."

I'd not set out to be kind, but his comment was arresting. I reflected on the countless number of people we interact with in the course of each day. So many of them are people with whom a simple transaction takes place. I could empathize, as none of us wish to be anonymous or invisible. It is a contradiction to the truth of being loved for our existence and being relatives of the Holy.

The following day, someone befriended me on Facebook and wrote with generous kindness about what I'd said in a talk he'd heard me give the night before. I was not looking for his kindness until I received it as the lovely unexpected gift that it was in my day. Kindness may not be a religion in and of itself, yet it is an expression of our journey to a new way of being human.

Kindness emerges from our mindfulness about being present and aware of those we interact with each day. I make it a practice to give thanks every day for at least one kindness received. As I listen to my own breath in daily meditation, present to myself and to the breath of life which flows through me, I become mindful about receiving and interacting with the kindness that exits around me at all times. At the same time, I invite the gift or blessing of kindness to be expressed with each person I encounter.

Your own interests or passions present you with the tools of kindness residing within you and waiting to be offered to others. Corkie is a woman in her 90s who delights in baking bread for her family and friends. She adores the way in which the aroma of bread baking in her oven fills her house, and it causes her pleasure to think of others enjoying the simple sustenance that emerges from the oven.

Much to her surprise, Corkie was deeply moved by her experience of meeting men and women who were homeless when she accepted an invitation to serve at a dinner given in their honor in her neighborhood. In the weeks that followed, she could not get the images and stories of the homeless out of her imagination. One day, she intuitively decided to bake a much larger batch of bread and take it as a contribution to a meal for the homeless. She was unprepared for the gratitude that the guests expressed as they finished every last piece of the loaves she provided.

Corkie decided that she would share her joy by baking bread for 100 homeless dinner guests each week. When I expressed my admiration for her generosity, she brushed it off saying, "Don't thank me; it's such a small gesture. It is just one thing that I can do." Corkie began to make sure that her deliveries of bread coincided with the arrival of the homeless dinner guests each week, and slowly she got to know the names, faces, and stories of those present for the meal.

Corkie's "small thing" was a gift anticipated with much expectation by those who gathered for a meal each week. More than delicious bread, Corkie's expression of kindness offered human connection of inestimable value to the guests, reminding them of their connection with the larger human family.

Similarly, the Universe invites you to share your joys and passions in ordinary acts of kindness. No act of kindness or generosity is ever too small a thing to offer. When you preclude your offering by assuming that it is not large or important enough, you exclude yourself and others from risky or unexpected invitations. Instead, allow yourself to be responsive to the flow of the Universe in which every joy and passion of yours is cause for celebrating with others.

We often bump up against the needs, wants, and expectations of others as we participate in polishing the world through acts of kindness. I received a phone call from Henry, who was calling not to talk, but to deliver an angry monologue about how I had disappointed him in a protest against police brutality directed toward peaceful protesters. Henry was convinced about how his clergy friend George would have responded. "Why didn't you lead people to lie down in front of the police cars? George would have!"

Henry did not know that George and I are friends with deep affection for one another—friends with very different gifts, approaches, and temperament. Before slamming the phone down, Henry declared, "You're certainly not George!" He was certainly correct about that, even if tersely dismissive of me. We've each thought or expressed disappointment about the response of others to polishing the world.

The real question is never about the other person. It is always about you. In doing what others want, you seldom shine. Your own unique gifts, temperament, personality, and circumstances are the context in which the invitation to polish the world is received. Your intuitive imagination will lead you in knowing how to engage in acts of kindness that shine light and hope on the lives of others.

Reflect:

- What difference does it make when you accept the risky invitations of life? What bliss will be birthed in you as a result?

- How will you choose to love and be loved unconditionally today? What will this mean for the human family?

- What truths will be revealed today, as you trust that you are part of limitless imagination? How will your actions reflect the imagination of the Holy?

Spirited Practices

- Name and give thanks each day for something about you that is loveable and cause for being loved for your existence.

- Write down each instance of your imagination leading you to accept a risky invitation.

- Invite each day to reveal to you the possibility of polishing the world in kindness and hope.

> The way is not in the sky. The way is in the heart.
> —Buddha

Pathway Four:
Home in Your Heart

"Flight 174 to Rio De Janeiro is now boarding at Gate 51!" The crackling announcement interrupted our conversation, reminding my parents and I that our only visit in the past two years was about to end. They were returning to Cape Town without me. New York was now my home.

My father stood there awkwardly, carry-on bag in hand. Clearly uncomfortable, he leaned toward me, his voice quaking with emotion. "I don't know when we'll be together again..." Tears filled his eyes, then mine. "I love you," he said quietly. And then, amid the swirling chaos that is JFK airport, my father kissed my cheek, and tenderly held my head.

I was thrown off guard by such emotion from a man who had not been raised to express demonstrative displays of feeling. It was a rare moment of emotional intimacy with my father. As I hugged and kissed him in return, I felt overwhelmed by this unexpected gift of immeasurable worth from him. "I love you too, Dad," I said as I wondered if I could stop a welling avalanche of tears of gladness and grief. I was filled with a nearly delirious gladness for what we had both just experienced. An expectant grief about losing future moments such as this one was accentuated by the repeated boarding call.

All around us, families were bidding their farewells. The lush cadences of many languages created a human symphony of love that transformed the departure lounge into a modern-day Jerusalem on the day of Pentecost. Against this pastiche of farewells, I reflected on our hearts as a human labyrinth of love, and wondered what it meant for each of us to leave part of our heart in one place.

By then I was at the boarding gate with my dad as he fumbled for his South African passport. Seeing the seal of that country was a reminder that I could not return to my place of birth without being imprisoned. Had I taken full advantage of the weeks together to savor being in the company of my parents or had I frittered the time away? Were there things left unsaid by any of us that I would regret?

As my father headed to the plane, he turned to wave. In that moment, the welling tears flowed down my cheeks. I took the hand of my mother, who was remaining with me for another week and we weaved our way through the throngs of people engaged in their own questions of memories and emotions embossed on their hearts. As we looked at the modern-day pilgrims in the terminal, we pondered aloud about the similarities between the journeys of American immigrants and journeys of the heart.

"Mom, do you remember our time at Plymouth Rock and Ellis Island?" I asked. She smiled and said, "Don't forget the Statue of Liberty. That longing for freedom is what brought people to America—and it's why you have a home here too." As we traveled back to my apartment, we reminisced about the other founding places of America that are like a shrine to the journeys that millions make, leaving behind their home and part of their heart in pursuit of freedom.

My mother smiled and reached for my hand as she said, "Your father and I miss you terribly. There isn't a day we don't talk and think about you. But we thank God every day that you are safe. Your friends here are wonderful. So, we're sometimes sad but mostly just happy. You'll come home someday, but this is your home now." As she said this, I marveled at the fact that, in less than two years, it felt like home.

The gladness and grief of my tears in the airport settled in as if they were becoming familiar companions in my heart. Both emotions felt true. I asked my mother about her childhood in Egypt and whether it was difficult for her to have emigrated. "The memories are always alive in my heart. Can you imagine we used to play on the Sphinx and clamber up the pyramids on Sunday afternoons? But my heart is with your father and our life together. And now part of our heart is with you in your home." I wondered if similar conversations were happening among those who had been with us in the airport lounge as they reflected on the coming and going that mark our journey and heart.

My father's kiss accompanied by his words of love staked a place in my heart and contoured my journey to becoming more fully human. My mother's reflections served as a witness to my journey and seemed to be a blessing on the unfolding, uncertain road ahead. Both were shining a light on the interconnectedness of the variety of people and places that allow the chambers of our heart to become home.

Home is a physical, emotional, intellectual, and spiritual destination. You can choose to live with segmented experiences of home, resulting in an unsettled, homeless way of life in which you are always searching for your one true home. Or you can choose the journey to a seamless experience of home by intentionally navigating the landscapes that shaped you. In this way, your life becomes a richly textured place of hospitality and joy—no matter what your circumstances, no matter where you live.

Like that kiss from my father, our lives are replete with defining moments that illuminate what is most dear in our hearts. These moments forge our experience of being at home with the many facets of who we are. They invite us to a new awareness and remind us that we are intended to live in harmony with a rich life-tapestry of people and places.

There are three stepping stones that beckon us to a new consciousness of being at home in our hearts as we travel the journey to becoming more fully human:

1. *Be present to your heart experiences—calling forth your true self.*

2. *It's not all about you—life beyond the litter.*

3. *The Reservoir of the Holy—your heart is the nourisher of life.*

Being at home in your heart is a dance for your life—a dance that leads you to discover and re-discover that your inexplicable, intrinsic value is discovered by being at home in your heart.

Stepping Stone One: Be Present to Your Heart Experiences

Your life journey is marked by the guideposts of an ever-deepening friendship with the Holy, yourself, and others, and illuminated by your willingness to go deeper and find your risk. How you are present to your heart shapes the contours of your risks and your humanity.

People Are Nice

Dwelling on the hurts or wounds inflicted by others robs us of a full heart experience. When we rigidly define ourselves by our wounds, we surrender our life to negative energy and a constrained, suspicious view of others. In the same way, embracing the truth that people are nice unleashes a life-giving energy.

In graduate school, I painstakingly cobbled together scholarships and jobs that allowed me to pay my tuition and living expenses. When I received notification that I had been awarded a scholarship that I had not applied for, I was astounded. As I thanked the professor who had nominated me, I asked why he had done this. "I grew up in a poor family in rural Mississippi where none of my relatives had graduated high school," he said. "When I went north to school, I was uprooted and struggled to pay the bills—not unlike you. A professor nominated me for a scholarship that changed that struggle, and when I thanked him he said his true thanks would be expressed by me doing the same for others. You're a nice guy with promise; be nice in the same way to others," he said.

In the Hebrew tradition, the heart is understood as the location and guts of our humanity. In the Sufi mystical tradition, the heart is both the seat of your intellect and the throne of the spirit. Within this throne of the spirit, your heart is like a mirror in constant need of polishing to remove the rust from the metal frame around the mirror. The rust is understood to be a reminder that when you forget the Holy in your mirror, you forget who you are intended to be. When you polish your intentional choices to see and experience the niceness present in yourself and others, you remember the Holy and the magnificence of your own journey.

Gloria experienced this through the unexpected gift of friends who knew that she was approaching a signature birthday. Arriving at their home for the monthly dinner they enjoyed with each other, her eyes filled with tears when she realized that a room full of people was there to celebrate her. Each friend had contributed stories and photos to a book expressing their love, appreciation, and admiration of her.

Gloria's abusive upbringing had led her to live with guarded emotions and little expectation for the niceness of others expressed toward her. Overwhelmed by the unexpected celebration, Gloria could have seen the outpouring of affection as a one-off event. Instead she found herself drawn by its invitation to a new awareness of being present to the heart experiences of her life and to those who allow her to be at home in her heart.

Gloria's thankfulness for what she experienced that day led to a new intentionality about life, beginning each day with mindfulness about appreciative awareness of each person she meets. Her practice includes thanking at least one person each day for some quality of goodness or niceness that she identifies in them. Gloria says, "It's changed my life and how I experience others and myself! Instead of guarded suspiciousness, I now live with a sense of awe about how we need one another. I delight in experiencing what happens in that moment of identifying something nice or good in another person—so many of us just don't expect it." Gloria has learned to be receptive to niceness identified in her by others and to appreciate her own capacity for niceness.

"My experience of life has shifted," she says. "I've discovered that my heart is more generous in how I approach each day." Like Gloria, you too will discover that the home you create in your heart expands as you live within the ecology of giving and receiving simple acts of niceness each day.

Every day you make choices about the consciousness and energy with which you approach the day. For instance, when you get up and launch into the day without intention, you surrender your mindfulness to the energetic forces around you and react to random experiences. You are then at the mercy of the day, and your capacity to experience people being nice is diminished.

When you welcome the well-being and happiness of each person, you experience an energetically transformative way to embrace each day. You engage with others differently. You discover that your consciousness and the energy of the Holy are invited to be in harmony and that niceness is allowed to breathe and be discovered. Your willingness to "meet the nice in others" impacts who you invite to companion your heart along the way.

Invite Heart Companions

We are made for oneness and family, yet "family" is a word that often evokes a myriad of images—some that include life-giving, nurturing relationships, and some that are abusive or stultifying. Your journey invites you to create a family of heart companions by proactively choosing enlivening relationships that go beyond the limitations of bloodlines or family-of-origin obligations. This is vital, as your heart companions mold your experience of being fully alive. Inviting heart companions into your journey is spirit sustenance for integrating the homes left behind with the new homes of heart and place.

I've discovered that Lucy, my Chocolate Labrador, is a heart companion who punctuates my days with generous reminders of what grounds my heart. When I am at work in my office focused on meeting goals or deadlines for the day, Lucy will come and put her head on my lap, inviting me to take her out for a walk or to play. I could see Lucy's needs as an interruption or obligation. Instead, I've learned that her gift reminds me to go outside, to breathe deeply, and to be awake to the beauty surrounding me outdoors.

Lucy's invitation to be re-grounded in the rhythm of each day is more than an affection and play break. This heart companion invites me to remember the heart companions who shape and form who I am. In Lucy's gifts, I am reminded to send an e-mail or place a call inviting a shared heart space with another person that day. Similarly, pay attention to the heart companions whom you might take for granted.

In my new home in America, my acute loss of family was heightened by the lack of the familiar—from items in a grocery store, to learning that it was all right to eat a hamburger with my hands. Yet in the hospitality of other South Africans living in New York, I discovered that others like me defined themselves by creating a cocoon to cherish their shared heritage and memories of home. In this way, they found comfort in the unfamiliar. Like the experience of many immigrant groups, true home was a place kept alive in their hearts. In some ways, this walled them off from fully engaging with those in their new country.

In any experience of being uprooted, you can be trapped by feelings of dislocation and a hankering for those with whom you are not physically present. Moving from one town to another, to a new country, a new job, or the ending of a marriage makes it tempting to define yourself by what you have left behind in the real or imagined loss of home, place, and people. It is a choice that closes chambers of your heart.

I discovered that it was not an either/or choice. Instead, it was an orientation of the heart that would allow me to create a wider circle of family. By choosing to intentionally invite heart companions into my life journey, I chose to define my life by looking outwardly with expectancy. This began a lifelong practice of intentional openness to the holy surprises revealed in encounters with others. As I set a dinner table for guests in my studio apartment or extended an invitation to walk in the parks of New York City, I found the sacred ground of meeting the heartfelt truth in others. Being at home in my heart was emerging in a seamless way.

Your Chamber of Love and Loss

Your loves and losses invite you to embrace and experience the truths that your sculpted heart reveals about being at home in the world with yourself. What terrified people about the person of Jesus was his relentless insistence that with tender luminosity we go ever deeper into the truth of our life. The places of love and loss invite that same tender luminosity from you.

The practice of detachment and letting go is an invitation into the luminosity that emerges when you are able to experience your loves and losses through new lenses. My friend Evelyn called to share the breathlessness with which she had discovered this truth. She said, "I've been down in my basement and saw with new eyes the box of hate mail sent to me by my former husband during our divorce. I've seen that box for 15 years but today I realized that I wasn't keeping the box so much as it was keeping me." It was a transformative awareness for Evelyn.

She could have chosen to ignore this new truth but instead chose to act on what it revealed. Evelyn described getting rid of the letters as a spiritual opening to becoming more fully alive on her journey. Several days later in a simple ritual of poetry readings and songs shared with her closest heart companions, Evelyn burned the letters and offered them to the Universe. As she detached from their presence, she offered intentions for the well-being of her former spouse and for herself.

Reflecting on this experience Evelyn said, "The part of my heart that had been locked up as securely as that box of letters was opened, freeing me to love more generously and to experience a more expansive heart. Instead of the ugliness of the letters framing my story, there is a new openness to how I'm able to receive myself, others, and the Holy."

Your own chamber of love and loss is never intended to imprison and enclose you. Instead, the wisdom of those experiences is revealed to you when you are able to detach and therefore see your own journey to a new way of being human through cleansed lenses. You then begin to live with a tender luminosity about your own self and others that is enlivening.

My sojourn with a literalist church resulted in my acceptance of an exclusive understanding of the Holy that blocked off the chambers of my heart. My wakeup call came from conversations with my maternal grandmother, Masha, in which it became clear to me that my involvement with fundamentalist religion was tearing me away from life itself. Surely this was the antithesis of spirituality, which is about the breath of life found in each of us.

Granny, as I called Masha, often expressed to me her loss and longing to see in the afterlife her first born child Marjorie, who died of influenza when she was six weeks old. This chamber of love and loss for Marjorie was never far from Granny's emotions. But it was her husband Robert—my grandfather—who was the focus of her most persistent questioning. He loathed organized religion and seldom missed the opportunity to roll down the car window as we passed a church on a Sunday afternoon drive to spit at it. "Surely God will have me be with both of them in heaven?" Granny would ask me.

"Only if they are born again" I offered repeatedly, sounding like the Holy's executioner and judge. Granny would dissolve into tears at the thought of the Holy having a heart of stone that would permanently condemn her to an eternal chamber of loss. I was quoting from the story of Jesus's encounter with Nicodemus who sought Christ out to ask what he must do on his search for truth. I had memorized the incorrect translation of the answer—to be "born again"—and internalized the presumption that only fundamentalists could adjudicate this litmus test. The correct translation of the word is to be "born anew."

Struggling with my own identity and place in the ecology of love, I discovered that the correct translation of Christ's answer is to be "born anew"—not "again." I began to appreciate the encounter between Jesus and Nicodemus as a tender and luminous one in which Nicodemus is the archetypal spiritual seeker who is willing to let go of his own rigid certainties and his assumed privileges of birth with the Holy. Jesus refuses to do Nicodemus's interior work for him, inviting him instead to be born anew in his own life. My heart leapt at this new insight about finding enlightenment in our search—not in declarative certainty.

Sharing my new insights with Granny, I expressed shame, regret, and sadness at having dared to presume judgmental exclusion. The tender invitational story about Nicodemus came to life between us as Granny and I cried together. I had come close to imploding her heart chambers of loss and love and to detonating a new chamber of such loss in our relationship. As she held me saying, "I love you, Robert," we entered into a transformed heart space.

If the first duty of love is to listen, then Granny and I were discovering that truth together. Instead of arrogant pronouncements, we began to go deeper into that tender luminosity that expands and heals the chamber of loss and love.

Stepping Stone Two:
It's Not All About You

The destination of your journey is never just you. As you find your risk, you discover that we each contribute to a gorgeous rhythm of love's dancing radiance. The rhythm does not reside in you by yourself or me by myself; it is a collective beat of our hearts.

The energy of the Holy is not discovered as solitary human beings; it is discovered in community that links your heart space with that of others. This enlivened way of being human flows from the choices you make about how to be alive in the world.

New Vantage Points

To love, to hold, and to let go is a sacred circular motion revealed to us as we appreciate the new vantage points that our journey brings. As I moved toward being more alive in the world, I discovered an invitation to a new perspective on my desire to create extended family—hidden in the debris of my life.

After years of making weekly phone calls to Shaun, a member of my new extended family in America, it became apparent that the conversations followed a familiar pattern of Shaun's grievances about the world and the unhappiness that an ever-changing array of people seemed to shower on him. Right on cue, I would suggest how Shaun could engage in a more life-giving way with himself and others. Eventually a new vantage point emerged as I noticed my increasing dread about these phone calls. With liberating relief, I finally asked myself, "Why are you falling into the role of saving or rescuing? Shaun's anger and unhappiness is toxic." Giving voice to the truth that un-reciprocal relationships are not relationships brought an epiphany to me. I thought of Jesus's concise wisdom for relationships—to love others, to do good, to be merciful, and to expect nothing in return. Except I was expecting something in return—I had been single-minded in assuming that Shaun would be part of my extended family. The life-giving and grounding quality of my belief in the primacy of relationships had a shadow side to it that I could only see through when the debris of my dissatisfaction clamored for my attention. I chose to detach from the relationship with loving mindfulness. I could continue to love Shaun and hold him in my heart, and simultaneously let go of my expectations and offer his well-being and mine to the Universe.

The new vantage point of engaging in intentional reciprocity with my extended family brought with it new heart energy. Shaun followed his own path to well-being, and two decades later we began to build a familial relationship that only the practice of loving, holding, and letting go could create space for.

Likewise, your vantage points will reveal choices for your heart energy. What do you see from here?

"Wake up!" is the singular and most significant revelation that reappears through the seasons of your journey appearing as an old, trusted friend shaking you up to unexpected vantage points on the new way to being human. When you wake up to a new vantage point, it is a moment of recognition of what is most significant, dear, and life-giving on your journey.

❖ ❖ ❖ ❖ ❖ ❖ ❖ ❖ ❖ ❖ ❖ ❖ ❖ ❖ ❖ ❖ ❖

An abrupt recognition presented itself to me when my spouse's grandfather died. Ken's death represented more than the ending of a relationship between grandchild and grandfather. Ken was the living link to my spouse's biological father, who was killed months before his birth. The graveside service was set for Christmas Eve, three hours away from where we lived in Seattle. It was an intensely busy day for me, with four Christmas services to lead that afternoon and evening. We jointly made the decision that I would not attend the funeral and believed that it was the right decision at that moment in time.

In the months that followed, a slew of recognitions presented themselves to me of gatherings with extended family and friends that I had missed or those that I had only dropped in on between work commitments. Those in the congregation I served were part of my heart, and I relished in my work that was deeply satisfying. The lengthy catalog of my personal life that I had missed out on was something that only I was responsible for in allowing such a packed and tightly controlled professional schedule to run my life. In my recognition, I realized that I was an interloper in my own life.

When recognition presents itself to you, it is accompanied by regret. Regret is the intentional mindfulness of the cost associated with the things we are doing or not doing—regret about the cost to ourselves and to others. On your journey, regret is a resting place—not a destination. Regret presented me with the choice of seeing with new eyes what my life looked like. Would my spouse and extended family continue to be fitted in to my schedule, or would I see this as an invitation to choose a more wholesome way of being? From the vantage point of recognition and regret I could choose to live as a victim of my schedule or do something about it.

Your recognition and regret bloom into a new vantage point when you choose to take the next step of reorienting your life. The reorienting begins with small, intentional, and deliberate steps, because you are on a journey, rather than overturning your entire life. I began to make seemingly small decisions about what to say yes or no to. It was a mindful approach allowing me to say no to life-draining habit energy, in order to say yes to creating space and time for life-giving habit energy.

When your new vantage point is entered through reorienting your life, you should expect that some people in your orbit will react with umbrage because you have upset their needs. Their actions or displeasure will be focused on you, but it is normally about them, and you cannot return to your pre-recognition without putting your own life at risk. Ironically, those who noticed and expressed the greatest disappointment or anger at my reorienting were people known for their emphasis on leading balanced and healthy lives!

The reorienting of my life resulted in entering more fully into a new way of being human that honors the ecology of the multiplicity of relationships with new awareness of the circle of life that they represent. Likewise, your new vantage points invite you to wake up to reorienting your life to explore the spacious chambers of your heart.

Life Discovered in the Shadows

The unexpected shadows that result from your freely made choices or those of the ones you love can distract you from seeing the path of being at home in your heart. The shadows invite you to rediscover the truth of heart spaces that bring you fully alive. They are choices that define your humanity.

My friend Grant's daughter Thandi had always been his pride and joy. As she prepared for college, this remarkable young woman was offered full scholarships to several of the most prestigious Ivy League schools in the United States. On her 18th birthday, Thandi announced to her parents that she had celebrated her adulthood by signing up to become a U.S. Marine. Grant experienced it as a hand grenade exploding in his life.

Grant's anger and confusion were matched by his disbelief. "Why is she throwing away the opportunity of a lifetime?" he asked. He wondered, "What have we done wrong as parents that Thandi would even consider joining the Marines?" In this shadowy space, Grant remembered the anger and disappointment of his own parents who refused to see or speak to him for seven years after he married a woman of color. "Am I going to repeat the cycle and live like a homeless person without my daughter in my heart space?" he asked.

During the course of many weeks, Grant struggled with the truth that he loved Thandi for her existence, and he expressed his deepest fear—"I'm scared that the Marines will knock out of her the very qualities that make her such a gorgeous person." Grant made a choice not to live in the shadows of his fears and preconceived notions and to love his daughter without condition.

At her Marine graduation, Grant said, "All of Thandi's magnificent qualities have been strengthened and are in full blossom. I was wrong; this could have been all about me, but instead I'm bursting with pride for her." The shadows of umbrage, righteousness, and confusion had given way to authentic conversation and emotions expressed between father and daughter because of the choices made.

When you live your life through the lens of another person, you end up clouding your own lenses, resulting in missing out on your own magnificence. Ginna spoke with envy and jealousy about the lives of her friends, resenting their vacations, homes, and relationships. Her barbs and innuendo about their lives had a sharp edge to them often disguised as humor. Several of those friends realized that they were withdrawing from time spent with Ginna and decided that they respected and valued her enough to challenge her behavior.

Ginna attempted to tell her friends that her comments about their lives were always made in jest, but they would not play along with the subterfuge. Ginna's appeal for their codependency was not what her friends had in mind with their intervention. The shadows that Ginna had chosen to live among led to her friends' willingness to detach from her and her behavior. As she settled into this truth, Ginna realized that it was a wake-up call inviting her to new choices about how to re-imagine being human.

Instead of choosing to remain distracted from her life Ginna worked with a guide and began to re-orient her life with her own self. Developing new attentiveness to the words she used, Ginna began to be mindful of the only life that she could be responsible for—her own. Replacing her envy and jealousy of others, Ginna took on the practice of naming at least one thing that she was thankful for in her life each day. After several months Ginna began to punctuate her day with meditation breaks, using words such as "gratitude" or "thankful." She said, "Repeating phrases such as these, I became present to the breath flowing through my body that invited me to remember that my life is profoundly bound up with that of others."

Ginna's new lenses led her to be aware of the beauty and magnificence that exist within her. In place of her longing for the imagined life and material possessions of others, Ginna began to cultivate a profound appreciation for the only life that she is responsible for. "The shifts have taken time," she says, "but I notice how different my relationships are because I have loving appreciation for me and my life." The shadows of the past have given way to discovering a new authentic way to be human.

Your journey depends on your willingness to move beyond your own shadows of certainty and into the invitation to find your risk with others. What will you find? And who will you love better as a result?

Multiplying Courage

Courage is not reserved for the heroines and heroes of our imagination. Heart and courage come from the same root word, mirroring the way in which they coexist in our lives. Multiplying courage for your journey to becoming fully human is discovered as you pay attention to others. Courageously allowing life to grow within you as your heart cracks open will prepare you to meet the unexpected heart spaces of others.

My friend Jolene and I were talking about her spirituality and its relationship to her work as a children's librarian. She said, "The luster of my life felt dimmed by the predictable routine of my job until I started talking with Alan." Alan was an amazing 12-year-old boy who sought refuge in the library every day.

One day, Jolene asked Alan what he would like to be when he grew up. She knew that his family struggled on the verge of poverty and lived in a sketchy neighborhood known for violence. Alan said, "I just don't ever think about that," and then added, "I don't think I'll live long enough for that." Jolene was jolted by the limited horizon that this 12-year-old assumed was normal; the luster of her own life suddenly appeared to be more radiant as she wondered about the level of courage Alan would need to imagine life beyond his teenage years.

Jolene quickly discovered that the survival mode of Alan's family offered little room for future thinking. The safe space of the library and the books that Alan loved became the setting for encouraging reading that would spark his imagination. As Alan began to imagine adulthood, his world was shifted by being held up at knifepoint and beaten by a group of young men outside his home. Alan and Jolene's courage was tested to exist beyond the life-threatening experience.

With breathless discovery, Alan came to Jolene one day to say, "The library is like a cocoon where I can imagine the courage to grow wings." Jolene's own heart space met the courage of Alan, who went on to graduate from high school and attend community college. They each experienced hearts cracked open, multiplying courage for their journey.

A gift exchange emerges when you live with awareness of the invitations to courage that your journey brings. What invitations have been extended to you? What gift will you bring?

Stepping Stone Three: The Reservoir of the Holy—Your Heart

Your heart is the reservoir of the Holy, a place of emergence drawing you to know that you are an abode of the sacred. To intuitively connect to your heart as you integrate the experiences of your journey and seek oneness with the many facets reflecting your splendor is a spiritual practice.

Everything Belongs

When self is the primary focus of your journey, you live with dissatisfying shadows of isolation and disconnect from your life. By contrast, the marker of the interior work drawing you to become more fully human is the way you choose to see the truth that your life is defined by a rich tapestry of relationships. It is a profoundly spiritual grounding in which you experience everything as belonging.

The creation and life of a mandala invited me into a new perspective of my own understanding of what it means to belong to everything.

Throughout the course of a week spent with Buddhist monks creating a mandala in a public space, replete with teachings about the significance of the mandala, I entered into the rhythm of their daily chants and prayers. The dazzling beauty of the mandala was revealed with each day's new addition to it. I discovered that the spiritual practices accompanying the creation invited me into the interconnection between all created things.

Although I knew how the week would culminate, I was unprepared for its impact on me. On the last day of the week, the monks chanted their prayers around the mandala while reverently and tenderly scooping it up into a vase. Before my eyes this work of beauty was reconfigured by the limits of the vase after which we journeyed to the shores of a nearby lake where the monks committed it to the waters with chants and prayers. The sadness I felt in letting go of the vaporized beauty gave way to realizing that my attachment to the images of the mandala would serve no other purpose than to imprison the gift it offered.

As I watched the mandala disappear into the waters, I awakened to the truth that the mandala's beauty was inviting me beyond my own sadness. The waters into which it flowed were waters of life, replenishment, and birth. As I listened to the chanting of the Buddhist monks at the water's edge, the interconnectedness of all things flowing together was more than an idea. Like their chants, you are invited to discover in your voice and imagination the radiance of interconnection that your own life and that of the Universe invites you to be aware of. Your heart space begins to expansively open into a more fulsome new way to be human.

As a child, I relished time spent on the beach with my father. A gleeful delight was present in him as we built resplendent sandcastles and dug holes in the sand along the shoreline. On the second anniversary of his death, I honored his memory by walking along Barefoot Beach in Florida. As I walked, I saw a sandcastle worthy of an award for its magnificence that seemed to say, "Come and play with me!"

My father had been very present in my dreams that week and this unexpected sandcastle appeared as a gift evoking a flood of memories of the hundreds of sandcastles that Dad and I built and bonded over. On my return walk, I was horrified to see a park ranger aggressively using his beach buggy to demolish the sandcastle. I thought of the parents and their children who had built it. I was fuming at this wanton aggression and violence.

Instead of stewing about this demolition I said, "Good morning" to the ranger. "So, you're getting rid of a sandcastle?" I was unprepared for his answer. "Everyone is asked to take down their sandcastles on this beach before leaving—it's a preserve and nesting ground for turtles. If a turtle comes to shore searching for a spot to lay their eggs they could walk into the sandcastle and get stuck in a hole and die. So we have to keep the beach level for these friends of ours."

How easily I could have kept walking and being consumed by the negative energy of imagining what the ranger was up to. Instead, my practice of stopping, asking, listening, and engaging revealed life-giving energy with the Universe. The ranger's compassionate clarity about the ecology of our inter-relatedness with the turtles was filled with the energy of our oneness.

Instead of an aching emptiness in my heart on the anniversary of my father's death, I was invited to see the reminder that everything belongs. Sea turtles, sandcastle builders and their castle, a ranger and his buggy, along with my memories of my father all met, deeply intertwined in my heart.

Likewise on your journey, how you chose to allow yourself to see the experiences that each day offers will affect your capacity to place your heart and life in the context of "everything belongs." It is a harmony of being that offers a blessing of oneness to you.

Learn to Ask

Learning to ask with comfort reflects the ease with which you are at home in your heart with yourself and others. Inability to ask is usually rooted in your own imagined unworthiness, fear of losing independence, and specter of being dependent on others—barriers that keep you from being at home in your heart. Instead of building a wall around your heart's invitation to go deeper, your journey to oneness depends on cultivating the practice of asking.

I arrived in the United States with two suitcases, $1,000, and the promise to be met at JFK airport by friends of Desmond Tutu. Their church welcomed me and set up graduate school interviews for me, all because Tutu had asked them to. As I cobbled together scholarships and a student job, they generously offered to provide the financial bridge to cover the balance of the costs. All I needed to do was ask.

Struggling with my inability to ask, I visited Hays, the pastor of the church, and said, "It is incredibly difficult for me to ask for support; it is at odds with everything ingrained in me." He smiled and said, "Admitting that is a huge step. Your life has placed you in a community of people; imagine it as a gift exchange." Responding to my puzzled look, Hays added, "Your being among us is a gift we learn from, and you hopefully learn from us—we need to be reminded that we need one another. We're able to offer financial support in gratitude for your being here—is gratitude so hard to live with?"

As I grappled with the implications of his words, I reflected on each of us being pilgrims and the striking image of the word from which it comes—*agrum*—meaning "through the fields." To be a spiritual pilgrim is to be in motion and community with others whom we choose or that life presents to us. My own discomfort and hesitancy about asking disturbed my comfort zone and led me to soul-searching the truth that we are made for connecting relationships. I was discovering what the journey through the fields meant.

You do not always feel privileged, safe, or worthy enough to ask, trusting or loved enough to ask. Yet your journey in the dance of asking is like your other practices—always unfolding and leading you deeper into the truth of who you are, discovered in the context of others.

To ask something of another reflects the mindfulness being cultivated in you. To ask is a sign of your self-awareness, of being aware of another person with whom you become awake to life in a shared heart space. To ask is to put yourself in the context of those you ask something of; asking is an act of faith and a spiritual practice whose mark is the delight you discover in the reciprocity of trust that emerges. To ask is to be reminded that in trusted relationships you discover all that you need for this season on your journey to becoming fully human.

Coming Home

Your life is a sequence of itineraries that keep circling you back to your heart space, revealing at each visit the deepening awareness that your pilgrimage through the fields of life has chiseled contours of loss and love in the chambers of your heart. Unlike tourists who simply visit places, you are a pilgrim risking to stop and go deeper into the meaning of coming home to yourself and others.

I was unprepared for my father's phone call—"I have a favor to ask of you" he said. "Your mother and I need you to come home." It was the year of Nelson Mandela's release from prison, which meant that all exiles could return to South Africa without fear of imprisonment or intimidation. In spite of my apprehension about what had really changed in the country, I knew that I needed to accept my father's request and go home to visit.

As the plane descended over the Stellenbosch Mountains, I sat looking out of the window with tears streaming down my face; on the approach to the runway, I could see the breathtaking Table Mountain, with the city of Cape Town snuggled up against its contours. I was smiling, laughing, and sobbing all at once. My anxiety about the trip was dissolving. The person next to me tapped my arm, inquiring if I was all right. "I am so happy, so relieved; these are tears of a decade of being away. It's okay to come home," I offered between the tears and laughter.

My father's boyish grin covered his face as he kept hugging me. "We love you; thank you for coming home. Things are different now." They certainly were. The oppressive country I had left was on a path to reconciliation, truth-telling, and discovering a shared humanity out of the debris of apartheid. The memory of our family home was replaced by the retirement community that my parents had moved to. Friends and family had all experienced change in their circumstances. In the decade that I been gone, my life had expanded significantly in creating heart space for an extended American family together with new spaciousness in which to come out. Going home made it clear that the physical and heart spaces of home had become more richly textured with the grittiness of life for each of us. Things were indeed different.

The moments of recognition revealed when you go home do not let go of you. You may ignore or bury them, only to discover their insistence in demanding your attention. With every itinerary home, you can choose to be a pilgrim whose heart is open to the griefs and joys of a real or imagined home that you have carried with you. As you stop clutching at home, you begin to see its blessings in the crevices and contours of your heart.

My return to the home of my birth revealed a multiplicity of homes— in relationships renewed and those that were no more; in the splendor of mountains and oceans that had shaped my imagination; in the coexistence of crushing poverty and opulence; in memories at the gravestones of my grandmothers, who had died while I was gone; in meals that had existed in my memory but were now transformed into communion with others. Each was a moment of recognition about my interconnectedness with the sensory, physical, and emotional heart spaces of home. Regret, longing, delight, gratitude, sadness, and elation each shed light on the truth that, in coming home, I would return to this home repeatedly from the new home I had in America. Each home belonged in the contours of my heart.

Years later, my spouse and I were faced with a surprising invitation. His father invited him to return to rural eastern Washington State to help run the family farming businesses. In accepting the invitation we knew that we would spend more of our time living on a farm than in Seattle. We would be returning to a home that my spouse had left decades before and a certainty that you could not go home. My enthusiasm was tempered with trepidation as I wondered where my stimulation would come from.

Although I have always thrived on being in nature, I had only ever lived in urban environments. With the move, I knew that a new reality and a new season in my life were beginning, and I wondered with a sense of expectancy what the Holy and the Universe would reveal to me. Life in a rural farming community was unlike anything I had ever experienced before, and the closest town of any size is a 30-minute drive away. In the first few months, the disconnections between what I had always known and what I was experiencing were challenging to my sense of being at home in physically, and in my heart.

With relatively easy access to our Seattle apartment, I could have allowed myself to become a sojourner in a displaced life. Instead, I discovered that my choice of mindset would determine how I received the gifts of this new cycle in our life together. My urban sensibilities have been joined by becoming awake to the dependence on nature's rhythms, which reveal the folly of believing that we are ever completely in control of life, but instead part of the flow of the great river of life itself.

When I shop the produce aisles, I now view the selections with new eyes and appreciation for the physical demands on those who work in fields and orchards along with the chain of others whose work delivers the goods so seamlessly to those aisles. My experience of each day is affected by the rhythm of life demanded by crop cycles and the impact of when sunrise occurs. I am awake to life in a way that I would never have expected if we had not accepted the surprising invitation to live in a new place that has become home. It is in the chambers of my heart that a new spaciousness and rich appreciation for family relationships has been revealed.

Likewise, you will discover new dimensions of being at home in your heart and life when you do not clutch at a predetermined notion of how life must be and instead allow yourself to respond to the possibilities of how life might be when you cultivate an open mindset. Being present to such surprises will allow you to enter the flow of the river of life, bringing you fully alive.

Going home is part of the rhythm of the sacred dance to your being fully alive and fully human. Your mindful settling into the truth revealed by each home allows you to move from clutching at life to living in its embrace. You become a participant in the ancient spiritual practice of enlarging your heart. Like walking a labyrinth, you approach your heart at the center of being grateful for the paths taken and those yet to unfold.

Reflect:

- How will your journey be transformed by cultivating awareness of your heart spaces?

- What will you do to integrate the many homes of heart, place, and people that have formed you?

- How will your life experiences bring you more fully alive as you pay attention to the dance of going home?

Spirited Practices

- Befriend your heart experiences by mindfully naming them. Your chambers of love and loss, the people who are nice, and your heart companions reveal invitations to new choices that will shift your journey.

- What is revealed in your story when life is not all about you? Share with a trusted person your yearnings to move beyond the shadows as you pay attention to others from new vantage points.

- How have you discovered the Holy emerging in the reservoir of your heart? What unexpected new life will you discover in going home, where everything belongs and your asking is a gift?

Everything in the universe has a rhythm;
everything dances.
—Maya Angelou

Pathway Five:
Thin Places—Holiness Disguised

"Is this what you'd like the diocese of New York to be known for—electing the first openly gay Bishop?" Tension spiked in the room as the members of the selection committee leaned in to hear my response. Their fear and anxiety was palpable.

Right on cue, another member spoke, "If you are elected, Lambeth will refuse your participation. Bishops from around the world will stay away." The once-a-decade gathering of Anglican bishops at Lambeth Palace was to happen the following year in 1998.

Another one of the committee chimed in, saying, "I really find these comments and questions offensive. We have not treated any other nominee in this way." Gratitude rose in my heart for her rationality, concern, and truth-telling. Some around the room looked sheepish or embarrassed—as others appeared defiant and resolute. At this point, my inclusion on the short list of candidates for the next Bishop of New York seemed unlikely, at best.

I immediately thought of the retiring Bishop, Paul Moore, his steadfast support of the ordination of women to the priesthood, and his feisty and courageous support of the first openly lesbian priest whom he ordained. "So this is it! They want a break from exploring the boundaries of who is fully included." I said to myself.

So why had I been chosen to interview?

As I pondered the possibilities, I looked out at the expansive view of the New York City skyline, thinking back to the congregation I loved and shepherded in Peekskill. A cavalcade of their faces appeared in my mind, representing what had become one of the most diverse Episcopal congregations at that time. It felt like a gift, reminding me of my grounding and joy. The butterflies in my stomach danced with excitement.

As if reading my mind, one of the members said, "Your leadership in Peekskill has transformed a congregation once believed to have little future. It is alive—and lively. Members of this committee appreciate and admire what you have accomplished." Sitting at the head of the table looking at the expressions of those present, I was sure there must be a "but" coming.

Aching sadness and tenderness toward those around the table surged within me as I responded. "I understand that there is fear about my nomination and election. Many of us around this table give our hearts and lives to building welcoming, inclusive churches. We know the deep joys and fears in building such communities. Regardless of who is nominated and elected, we will continue to work for love that includes and celebrates every human being."

In the events that unfolded in the following weeks, I was challenged to be equally tender toward the fears I confronted in my own heart and mind. My relief at learning that I was not on the official slate of four nominees to be presented to the electing convention was upended by the phone calls I received. "We'd like to nominate you by petition from the floor," was the thrust of the message.

"If you allow your name to be put on the ballot you will be publicly out front on the issue, and make a statement about your sexuality" counseled my friend Bill. I knew he was right. "If you don't," he added, "those with less than charitable motives will go after you with laser-like precision."

The face of fear was now my own.

In the middle of the night several weeks later, I woke up to find my sheets soaked with sweat. Panicked, I leapt out of bed. As I turned on the lights to change the sheets I remembered the scriptural advice to not be anxious about earthly things. I smiled at myself, thinking, "Your fears and anxieties are no less real than those of the search committee!"

The next day I met with my spiritual guide, Paul. "Paul, these night sweats might be a wake-up call for me," I offered. With luminous, gentle clarity, Paul remarked, "Your life journey is about striving for integrity and wholeness. I love you for that and for the steps you keep taking. This is like a veiled meeting place for you and God. Perhaps even for a transformed, free you."

Paul's tender encouragement was my invitation to freedom.

In the days that followed, I recalled my pilgrimage to Celtic sites in Scotland and northern England. The Celts believe that there are two texts of scripture. One is the written holy text, and its companion is the text of Creation—the borderlands where God, nature, and self meet in what they call the thin places. The thin places are an invitation to intimate tenderness with our selves, the Holy, and Creation.

On this pilgrimage, I'd seen many visual presentations of the favorite Celtic image of Jesus's beloved disciple resting his head on Christ's breast. The tender intimacy of the image kept recurring in my imagination, offering me an invitation to be just as courageous and truthful. My life was on the line. I could choose to be consumed and overwhelmed by the shadowy presence of my anxieties and fears. Or, I could accept the invitation to the thin place to meet the Holy and myself with new eyes.

I called Paul and said I believed his response to me was opening up a pathway. "Never again do I want to be a prisoner to the fear of someone using who I am as a weapon," I said. Then I added, "Paul, I think the night sweats are leading me to a thin place of new union with myself and the Holy."

❧

What is a thin place? The thin places are found in nature and on the edges of your own fear and resistance to being fully alive. They form a veil through which you experience glimpses of the sacred. They offer an invitation to step out of the shadow places of our lives into transformation, resulting in oneness with yourself, the Holy, others, and nature.

You can choose to live defined by the particular shadows lurking in your life. They will reel you in, keeping you in a confined, cramped space on your journey. Like the dull, bored existence birthed by a bad relationship, your shadows can have their way with you, leading you to believe that hiding is a normal way to endure life. This is not what you or the world needs from your unique life. When the curtain is pulled back on your shadows, a new, more luminous truth is revealed about you and the freedom that your journey demands.

Here are three stepping stones to help you utilize the thin places as a spiritual positioning system on your capacious journey to becoming more fully alive.

1. Create mindful, aware living—to live your life open to the thin places.
2. Discover the disguises of the Holy—to be present to the surprises of the Holy around us.
3. Polish your connection to the Universe—to be grounded in your belovedness.

Stepping Stone One:
Create Mindful, Aware Living

When you create a life path of being mindful about your life and the Universe, you experience an awareness of living that takes you out of the shadows and beyond blame and victimhood. With spirit practices to ground you, you are then able to befriend the fears that could otherwise throw you off-balance. Your ensuing awareness allows you to be present as an active participant in your life.

Cultivating Awareness

In my experience with the nominating committee, it would have been easy to cast blame on their paranoid fears, or to focus on the disconnect between their affirmation of my leadership, and their refusal to imagine a wider possibility of that same leadership. Those questions were all worth engaging. The fuller story, however, invited me to discover why their reactions mirrored my own avoidance of the very same questions. I was being invited to cultivate awareness.

My growing awareness revealed that I could choose to be a victim or I could become a participant in what was being revealed in the beauty of my own life and story. I decided to choose the journey to a porous and often fragile borderland where all of who I am could encounter the generosity of the Holy. In that thin place, I discovered a robust fullness about my place within my story—and within the Universe.

Your own life, story, and being are of incalculable significance to you—and the world. In choosing to participate in the world as the gift that you are, you cease to be a victim. This spiritual paradigm shift away from victimhood makes it possible to travel to the thin places, and to shift the energy you choose to engage. So often your energy is expended trying to change others or modify their behavior, resulting in a subterfuge that keeps you from being fully alive. When you cultivate self-awareness around your intuitive reactions instead, you forge a path to creative, life-giving energy.

When we are on the cusp of an emerging awareness, the dislocation or eruption that manifests itself is messy and unsettling. To help me move through the dislocation in the weeks leading up to the interview, I wrote each day in my journal, expressing every hope and fear present in me. However, it was only after the interview that I grasped the level of awareness revealed in my daily spiritual practice of writing.

For example, my own disappointments about the conversation with the nominating committee were real. It was an unsafe environment in which I felt both the need to guard and protect myself as well as tenderness in hoping that the surreal nature of the meeting would be one that others would never have to endure. That awareness later presented itself in night-waking sweats of anxiety and fear about speaking the truth of who I am. Even so, cultivating awareness is never intended to make you feel bad. Your regrets and disappointments are what trap you in the sheer enormity of your emotional reactions.

The journey to the thin places is often scary, because in meeting the shadows that keep you from being fully alive, you are invited to actively participate in transformation that wakes you up to be more authentically human. My life was on the line. Yours is too. Choosing a companion guide to help you navigate your fears can often make the difference between allowing yourself to be kept in a holding pen or not. Choose accordingly!

Befriending Fear

The first casualty of fear is truth. Your fears hold you back, chaining you to a past that does not want you to move on. Often the fuel of catharsis, fear results in pretending to be alive, when in fact your life feels quite listless or dead. My night sweats were my body's way of saying "Wake up! Pay attention to what life is revealing!" I spent a lifetime navigating my service in an organization where the full truth of who I am was not always safe to reveal. I was out about my sexuality to some, but not to all. I justified this by taking comfort in the work of building inclusive, open congregations. My own need to be loved and to continue doing the work I adored collided with the construct of fear residing deep in my consciousness.

Up to that point, normalcy for me meant attempting to make peace with my fears. In the process, I succumbed to the voices who said my fears were justified. The unexpected gift of the meeting with the nominating committee resulted in knowing that I no longer wished to live with a "peace" that was not peace. The real meaning of peace is about seeking the well-being of all. The thin place was inviting me to embrace well-being and wholeness for myself, not just for others.

As I began to name my fears—of losing my job, of being rejected and denied the work I loved, of forfeiting some collegial relationships, of rejection as a community leader—a new truth dawned. The fears were related to my work—my family and friends who loved me as I am were not on the list! With this awareness, the fears began to lose their power over me. Their life-draining energy began to give way to a life-giving energy that allowed me to imagine the freedom of no longer walling-off part of myself.

I discovered that even as I detached from my fears, I befriended them. One day I said to my spiritual guide, "I wonder why this befriending of fear has taken so long for me?" As he smiled at my question, I added, "It feels like a cocooning has been going on in the buildup to this. I look back at recent years and realize that I've been nurtured with courage. It's as if I've been preparing to be birthed in the next steps along my journey."

Befriending fear in the thin place brought with it a cycle of death, re-birth, and a greater fullness of being alive than I ever imagined. I was not responsible for the reactions of others. I was only responsible for speaking the truth with a heart grounded in love and compassion. Likewise, you will discover as you befriend your fears that any death that occurs to self is always accompanied by rebirth.

Choosing to be aware of the thin places in your life directly correlates to how you befriend your fears about where the thin places will point you on your journey. Paying attention to the quiet, still voice within you along the way is a grounding practice for attention to the Holy within you.

Edward was my roommate at a week-long retreat. Each morning, I would hear him quietly singing a different song as he showered or when we hiked the grounds of the conference center together. I knew that Edward was under fire at work and that the he had endured significant losses in the previous years. I asked him about his singing. "I've done it for years," he said, "But it has taken on new significance in the last few years. I'm often surprised by what I sing. I've come to believe it is the quiet still voice, the sacred in my breath, reminding me of my compass for the day ahead."

Edward could have chosen to ignore that voice within and be consumed by stress, loss, or anxiety. He embraced singing as an intentional practice instead. Rather than an escape from the issues he was dealing with, the quiet voice within discovered through song connected Edward to the Universe and grounded him in life truths for the journey ahead. Instead of living reactively in response to fear about the present and the future, Edward befriended those fears by diminishing their power. "I'm aware of the truth of the turmoil I'm dealing with, yet there is a calm, grounded way of living that I have never experienced before," he said.

Likewise, when you choose to detach from or befriend your fears, the awareness of truth in your life is seen through different lenses. Rather than trying to banish your fears, you begin to experience them as an invitation, to be present to the thin places. When you ignore the invitation you do so at your own peril. You live your life in suspension. When you accept the invitation, the Universe and the Holy cheer you on. As you do so, you discover that the thin place is filled with life-giving truth and wisdom, and that courage, tenderness, and hope enfold your next steps along the path to a new way to be human.

Being Present

When I am present to myself I actively participate in the birth and rebirth of my oneness with others, myself, and the Holy. Each practice of being present invites a life-giving energy into my life and consciousness, giving me courage to visit or linger in the thin places.

I have a ritual of lying on the ground on my back, luxuriating under the night sky. In those moments, enfolded by the earth and the sheltering sky, I am reminded of my own place within Creation. In my moments of transition or entering a thin place, this ritual beckons me with a vivid reminder that the Universe itself is still creating whether I can see it or not. In the presence of dazzling stars, I become present to the same truth of creation being birthed in me.

The practice of presence is not limited to oneness with the night sky. It's possible to be present to life anywhere—at a farmer's market, on a New York subway, in an urban park, or sitting at a coffee shop. You can recalibrate your agenda, inviting awareness of the grandeur of ordinary moments.

My friend William relies on attending a one-hour religious service each week to be present. He works in a company that places significant pressure on him and his colleagues to produce. He says, "I feel trapped by the promises of financial reward. There is a gnawing inside of me to do different work, a yearning to listen to my passions, a longing to use my imagination and voice." William says that his one hour each week reminds him to be present to those truths. He clings to this, his lifeline of being present.

The gnawing, persistent questions that will not let you go are a reminder to cultivate awareness, to befriend the fear that challenges your acceptance of what is "normal." The questions keep inviting you to be present to your life. In their confluence, you ready yourself for the thin places as you create mindful, aware living.

To be present to the only life for which you are fully responsible—your own—cultivates awareness of the invitation that the thin places offer and shifts your awareness of the Universe and its generosity. The world needs this polishing from you. Your life is not intended to be all about you. A new way to be human encourages the expansion and sharing of the wisdom, delight, compassion, and generosity within you.

My friend Rudy rejected the single-minded focus on heaven or the afterlife that the religion of his youth obsessed about. He found instead that being present to the magnificence of his life allowed him to be present to others, and that his deep interconnectedness with the Universe was an experience of all that his childhood religion yearned for in their lust for the beauty of heaven. All of those longings were to be experienced in the present rather than putting the present on hold and imagining that life would be fulfilled in some unknown future.

Rudy respected the different path that his mother Ruth had chosen and honored the experiences of her last days before dying. Lying in a hospital bed in an intensive care unit, Ruth was unable to speak and used pen and paper to communicate to him the images she had experienced of God. She had seen a place with lakes and flowing rivers around which there were homes. Among the people in the houses, she saw her firstborn son, Greg, who had died when he was 10 years old. Ruth died the following morning. Several years later Rudy's daughter, who had converted to Mormonism, called to ask for his permission to rebaptize Ruth and Greg.

"Here's what I know," said Rudy to his daughter. "Your uncle and grandmother know a lot more about heaven than any of us. I also know that they're at a lake. So you do whatever you need to, but I don't think Grandma and Greg would be happy if Saint Peter suddenly appeared to them and said, 'You're out of here; you're moving to another heaven.'"

Rudy was disturbed by his daughter's understanding of competing heavens and her belief that rebaptizing the dead brought with it travel documents and visas to relocate. He said, "I know the Holy to be defined by generosity and love, and not by a mean-spirited exclusivity. My daughter needed to do be at peace with her beliefs. To engage in a dispute with her would be to remove myself from being present to life in the now."

Similarly, those around you will often seek to engage you with actions and conversation that distract you from being present to your life. This life-draining energy subtly disrupts and distances you from choosing the thin places that are revealed when you are present to your life and the Universe. Your life and that of others depends on your mindful choices. Intentionally choosing the life-giving energy of being present is your spiritual positioning system for becoming fully alive on a new way to being human.

Stepping Stone Two: Discovering the Disguises of the Holy

You and I are each one of the many disguises of the Holy. This is an anchoring truth on our quest to becoming fully human.

The Holy disguised in you shifts the ground on which your journey is revealed, inviting you into a generous way of encountering yourself and others, and unfolding the ever-deepening invitation that you are made for love and compassion.

This is no small truth. It will unsettle you at times because your assumptions, prejudices, fear, hopes, yearnings, and expectations will yield to a more porous spirituality. The disguises of the Holy are often where the thin places invite you in, providing a spiritual positioning system.

The Holy in You

Becoming fully human means that spiritual truths are revealed not in the abstract, but in the specificity and complicated wonder of who you are right now.

My naming and claiming of the truth of my sexuality was a watershed experience. I'd always believed that the Holy loved me—but this was different. Now I had to take notice of how the Holy is present in me as a gay man. The depth of this truth came from the unexpected "gift" of the nominating committee who unknowingly offered me a sacred time to pause and to be present—even as it opened me to seeing this truth in the lives of others.

My friend Cyndi spent years working with girls and young women from the Southside of Chicago to develop their leadership skills, claim their voice, access education, and learn to be community organizers. They were women typically overlooked because of their circumstances. Cyndi delighted in her work. She would often say, "You won't believe what I learned today from one of the women!" as she expressed amazement at their accomplishments. Occasionally, she spoke in spiritual language about seeing the image of the Holy revealed in those she worked with.

I admired Cyndi for her work and adored our friendship. She served as a midwife, helping to birth new life in others, even as she lived with terminal illness. In the days leading up to her death, her body ravaged by multiple cancers, her playful spirit and passion shone through in concise observations. I was unprepared for what she said on one of those final visits. "I've always believed that God is found in every person," she said, struggling to speak, "But I've never believed it about me." I was surprised and caught off guard by what followed. "Until today—today I know the Holy is found in me."

Cyndi was an icon to many, pointing to an expansively inclusive and generous way of being alive. Her empowerment of others was a gift. Yet it was Cyndi who needed to journey to her newfound truth about being one of the disguises of the Holy. At first I grieved that she could only luxuriate in this large truth in the final 48 hours of her life. Then I realized that her epiphany was like a blessing on her journey.

What is deepest in us, and most significant, is the magnificence of the Holy's disguise. I was as unprepared as Cyndi for this earth-shifting revelation in my life. It is the thread that shimmers through our interconnectedness with others and the Universe, casting light on the thin places.

When your consciousness acknowledges that the Holy is discovered in others as much as in you, life shifts. "Why do you always insist on saying Namaste to me?" Steven asked his friend with great annoyance. "Because I believe it's true—the Divinity within me adores and greets the Divinity within you" said his friend.

Through their conversation, Steven discovered that this tradition practiced by Sikhs and Hindus, among others, acknowledges the spark of the Holy within every person. Steven could have chosen to remain annoyed at his friend, but instead chose to see an invitation in the word that had frustrated him. He began to practice greeting a few people with Namaste, knowing that it means "I bow to you." In the ensuing weeks, Steven discovered that word is often unnecessary because the physical bowing gesture of Namaste expressed its intent.

As he practiced bringing his hands together at the heart, closing his eyes, and bowing to the person he was greeting, Steven began to experience transformation. He said, "The gesture engaged my intentions, my body, and my heart energy in ways I would never have imagined. Every time, I could feel the love of the Holy and the Universe flowing from my heart, and when another person responded in the same way, our oneness was tangible." The gesture spoke more powerfully than the word "Namaste," revealing to Steven a circle of honoring in which the flow of heart energy invited each person to meet the other on a field of compassion.

"I've discovered that this simple practice reflects and deepens what I believe about how interdependent our lives are," said Steven before adding, "It's opened an enclosure that I didn't even know I lived behind. It's opened my life and my heart to a fuller way of being human."

Your own life and engagement with the Universe shifts when you become awake to the truth that the sacred or Holy is found in every person. To live as though your life is only about you and those in your immediate circle becomes impossible. Life is changed. Your experience shifts. The field of your life becomes open to the thin places revealed in the unexpected meeting ground with others. In this gift, you realize that bowing to the sacred invites engagement with the world through acts of compassion, justice, love, and hope.

A chamber of mirrors is revealed to you when you honor the Holy in you. The mirrors of every life shimmer with that reflected image, celebrating a new way to be human within the interconnectedness of all of life.

Holy Surprises

The path to becoming fully human and fully alive is about more than your own journey. Your willingness to see the Holy revealed in the life of others orients and enlivens your heart with the surprising discovery that those to whom you have paid little or no attention are precisely the teachers you need for your journey. It is a repositioning of where you fit into the human story, a transformation that takes you to the thin places. It is also a place where assumptions and biases are challenged, often resulting in necessary loss.

❧ ❧ ❧ ❧ ❧ ❧ ❧ ❧ ❧ ❧ ❧ ❧ ❧ ❧ ❧ ❧ ❧

Edward was a wise mentor to me. In his heart, he believed that every person was a tabernacle of the Holy, and his love for the Christian practice of Holy Communion or Eucharist was striking. He liked to say, "If I honor Christ in the sacrament with my genuflecting, I should also genuflect to every person I pass on the streets." It gave new meaning to the greeting of Namaste used by Buddhists, Jains, and Hindus that literally means, "I bow to you," or "The light in me honors the light in you."

Edward struggled with a necessary loss. As a priest in the Episcopal Church, he dedicated much of his life to building an intentional relationship with the Russian Orthodox Church—until his church's decision to ordain women to the priesthood ruptured those relationships. Though he was in his 70s, Edward seriously considered leaving his church and tradition because this change meant that gender was no longer a determination of value, role, or function.

Turning to his own tradition to make sense of what he described as new debris all around, he discovered a surprise. He said, "I kept thinking of all those babies I baptized. We welcomed them unconditionally. We celebrated that they were full members of the church." He asked, "Are these rites a generously lavish embrace or a sham? How can I now say to the girls we baptize, 'Sorry, but you are really not a full member'?" As we spoke that night he told me, "The bishop has asked me to form a small class to train and prepare some of you for your ordination. He wants me to teach you how to celebrate the sacraments." I smiled at the thought of learning from his wisdom as I prepared to be ordained. Then he added, "The bishop wants four of you to be part of the class—and two of the four are women."

Edward was invited to see this loss and the resulting debris in a new light through the very sacraments so central to his spirituality. As we met weekly throughout many months, Edward was honest about his struggle to reconcile the new reality of women being ordained with his belief about each person being a tabernacle of the Holy. When our time came to be ordained, Edward was one of those presenting each of us to the bishop for ordination. He said to me, "The losses and the debris surrounding me made way for a feast I'd never imagined." Then he added, "My lenses have been cleaned. The whole idea of genuflecting to a person is reimagined."

Your daily life presents opportunities for discovering the Holy reimagined and revealed through an unexpected person—and to see yourself through new lenses. The veil of a thin place where the sacred meets life gives way to a new meeting ground with yourself and others.

Seeing With New Eyes

I clean my glasses several times a day, and I am always amazed at how they attract dust, finger marks, and dirt. When I put on my freshly cleaned glasses, I almost feel like I'm seeing with new eyes. In the same way, the lenses through which you approach life are also in constant need of cleaning. Through the sacred spaciousness offered by your daily spirit practices, you can approach life with the intention of seeing every circumstance with new eyes. In effect, you create a roadmap that prepares you to see the invitation to thin places in your life.

Preparing to cook for a family celebration, I noticed how unsettled I felt about preparing the meal and the party that would follow. There had been a significant family dispute the previous day between some who would be guests at my table. Instead of gladness about the evening, I felt anxiety. As a result, my usual practice of mindfully naming, visualizing, and thinking about each guest was blocked, along with the oneness and expectancy that this practice creates. Discovering the disguises of the Holy in my dinner guests seemed like a murky prospect.

I knew I could not fix relationships that needed repair. Instead, I chose to clean my "inner lenses" by meditating and visualizing, using one of the many names for the Holy found within each religious tradition. The variety of these names offered a window into the disguises of the Holy, and invited me to see beyond the images I most cherish.

As I chopped, sautéed, and cooked, I visualized and played with a few of those names: The One Who Plays and the Flute Playing God from the Hindu tradition, the Nourisher from Islam, the Sikh Destroyer of Fear, the Christian Lover of Souls, and the Jewish God of the Womb. These playful, nurturing, and tender images created a space in which I could return to my mindful anticipation of each guest.

That evening, my anxiety gave way as I saw with new eyes something magnificent, endearing, or inviting in the touch, conversation, or laughter of each guest. Even in the tension that lurked between those relationships needing repair, I saw cracked hearts opening to one another, revealing glimpses of the Holy.

Your intentions about the lenses through which you experience life determine your expectancy about living each day in the present. How will you think about each person you will meet in the course of the day?

My colleague Shannon describes herself as an introvert and says, "For years, I lived each day with a low-level anxiety, dreading too many encounters with other people." Although she was accomplished at learned extroverted behavior in her professional life, she said, "I felt like a fraud. I wanted some new way of being authentically engaged with other people. I no longer wanted to view people as disruptive interruptions in my day."

In her pursuit of spiritual wisdom, Shannon was intrigued by the Hindu view of unannounced guests whom they call *atithi*. For Hindu's, the atithi is to be treated as if she or he is a god. She also discovered that within the Christian tradition of Benedictine spirituality, a similar practice holds center stage, in which the person who appears at your door or before you is to be treated as if they are the Holy or the Christ.

Wondering if these insights were theoretical rather than practical Shannon decided to practice them in her daily encounters for several months. She began each day by inviting herself to be present to the Universe by asking to be a blessing to those she met and to receive a blessing from each person she encountered. Shannon was taking steps toward transformation by becoming aware of the unexpected gift of another person.

After three months of engaging in this practice, Shannon said, "The core of how I understand myself has begun to shift. My willingness to experience others as a god or the Holy changed how I engage with the person I am with, and in the process, I no longer identify myself primarily as an introvert. I still need the quiet alone space that introverts crave, but people have ceased to be interruptions and have instead become guests in my day and my life, for which I give thanks."

The choices you make about viewing life shape how fully alive you choose to be on the journey to a new way to be human. Your lenses will either keep you from or allow you to see the thin places of sacred meeting ground on your journey. Choose wisely because your life in the now is at stake.

Stepping Stone Three: Polishing Your Connection to the Universe

Each day you make choices about where you place your life and your story. In times of economic, emotional, or physical turmoil, it is tempting to face inward, make judgments, and hide within what you think you already know. This leads you to become a refugee from your own life. When you choose instead to place your story and life within the ecosystem of the Universe, you allow the thin places to breathe—and to be discovered.

The Guru Within

The sacred and holy exist within you. This truth reveals a potentially disruptive innovation you may have been taught not to believe—that the Universe and Holy live in all realms, not just realms above or beyond.

I was on a flight from Newark to Seattle. My companion and I were in the middle and aisle seats talking with Cynthia, the passenger in the window seat. She asked what I did for a living. I said, "I am a spiritual teacher who leads workshops and writes." She lunged across my companion in the middle seat and grabbed on to me exclaiming, "A holy man!" Despite her unusually demonstrative and unexpected response, we spent the remainder of the flight talking.

Her exclamation about a "holy man" was not about me. Cynthia was yearning to find trusted, authentic, and grounded guidance on her quest to integrate her career and personal life with a seamless, transparent spirituality. She is not alone in that search. Cynthia wanted to be a participant who assumes responsibility for her spiritual journey.

Along with millions of others, Cynthia found her experience of the "one size fits all" answers of her childhood religion to be stultifying. Those whom she had elevated to guru status along her journey were often opaque. Despite Internet resources that expanded her knowledge, she still hungered to integrate the realities of her life—including anger, doubt, resentment, and disillusionment—in her quest to become fully alive. In one of our subsequent conversations Cynthia said, "Instead of looking in the realms beyond for answers, my own life is a mediator of the wisdom traditions usually claimed as exclusive ground by 'experts.' It's like discovering a guru within."

Like Cynthia, I have discovered that when all of my authentic self—including those aspects of my life that confuse or bewilder me—are engaged with transparent light, the wisdom of the Universe and Holy is revealed and engaged—along with the wisdom of religious guides and tradition. Likewise, as you recognize the guru of wisdom within, you too can experience a seamless spirituality birthing you to become fully human.

Nurturing, developing, and blossoming the guru within invites attentiveness about how you care for yourself. And yet, such care never happens in isolation from other people. As you pay attention to what life and the Universe offers to you, beware of how easily your unexamined choices and routine can keep you walled off from the guru within. Be prepared to love yourself through choices that allow the guru to blossom.

A hectic day reminded me of how we make such choices in the rhythm of each day. I'd had one of those crazy overscheduled days with writing deadlines to meet and back-to-back appointments. That evening, I was leading a workshop at one of my favorite Unity congregations. Was I going to attend the meditation service that preceded my workshop, or would I use the time to catch up on some e-mail responses? I was surprised by the intuitive pull to attend the meditation.

I could have chosen to stay in and get up-to-date on e-mail. Instead, I listened to my intuition inviting me to self-care and the nurture of my spirit, and chose to participate in the meditation. The stresses of the day dissipated into the movement, breathing exercises, chanting, and intentions of the 40 minutes. Paying attention to my body and the Universe became an expression of loving myself and the guru within enough to enter into the oneness facilitated by the meditation. My connection with a community of people who had made similar choices that night was just as important. We each loved ourselves enough to nurture the guru within us by acknowledging that the journey to becoming fully alive is one of profound interconnection.

In listening to my intuition, I allowed it to trump my assumed plan for the evening and to reveal once again my need to pay attention to what the day revealed to me. The interactive reciprocity of the workshop reminded me that my choice had consequences that pointed far beyond me to the sacred hoop of life we all share.

Likewise, the guru within you does not exist in a vacuum to be turned on or off at will. Pay attention to it. Your intuitive and mindful choices nurture the wisdom that exists within you, thereby allowing you to be an active participant with others on the journey to a new way of being human.

Surprised by Love

The Universe and the Holy invite you beyond disillusionment into the blessing of being surprised by love. Yet it is easy to be trapped in the widely held paradigm that love is about "making nice." This set-up for failure, discontentment, and anger keeps you fenced-off from transformative, life-giving love. When you instead choose to be part of the Universe's ecosystem of love, your consciousness is given an opportunity to shift.

One night after a meeting, I sat on the edge of the bathtub, sobbing. For almost two years, a handful of people had tried everything they could imagine to make me leave my job. All attempts to reconcile with this small group went unreciprocated. That night, I had been relentlessly "charged" with being too charismatic a leader, too skilled at fundraising—and too powerful.

The temptation in such circumstances is to judge those who have ripped open their inconsistencies, and to wallow in the reality of pain, loss, or desire for revenge. I knew that unless I worked through those truths, they would become the defining container that incarcerated me. My disillusionment became a blessing rather than a scarring curse when I discovered that my physical reactions and truth-telling pointed to an invitation.

The sobs that contoured their way throughout my body cleansed and awakened me. It was a defining moment. Suddenly, I understood that the charges were not about the qualities of my leadership. I realized instead that my desire to reconcile had turned into an extended dark night of the soul. My health and place in the ecosystem of the Universe needed to be set free by relinquishing my cherished belief in the possibility of reconciliation.

I was surprised by love.

In the healing that followed that experience, my spirit practices sprung to new life. In that process, I discovered the sound of great silence. The great silence is the practice of letting go of your internal conversations with yourself, or the trap of incessantly reliving old stories. Instead, you look and listen to nature and life around you with a mindset of expectancy. It is a way of being present to the now. As I walked along shorelines, through an orchard, or an urban park, familiar landscapes beckoned me to pause, as if to say, "Please, please look at me! Look and listen!"

As I looked, the great silence was filled with sounds of birds, water lapping on a shore, or fruit dropping from a tree. The Universe seemed to be saying, "Remember your oneness with us. Step beyond those charges and be re-charged by re-entering your place in the fragile ecosystem of Creation." As I looked and listened, the thin places invited me in to be surprised by love revealed anew in the familiar.

As you are surprised by love, you will find a new appreciation and tenderness toward yourself and a generosity of spirit and wisdom from friends and mentors. Your journey of being present with the great silence will lead you to the thin places of renewal.

Open Mindset

Often consumed by meeting goals or perfecting the art of multi-tasking, I am aware that my laser focus on accomplishments or daily survival creates a closed mindset that leaves little time for remembering who I am or why I'm here. Life is designed to be a slow dance with the Holy in becoming fully alive, fully human—a porous space of open mindset where I meet myself and others.

I have always been an urban person who thrives on being in nature. When my spouse, Jerry, and I decided to spend much of our time living on his family farm in the high desert of Eastern Washington about three hours from Seattle, I was unprepared for the impact on my mindset. With trepidation I wondered, "Where will my stimulation come from?"

As we settled in, I doggedly clung to my urban mindset with frequent trips back to Seattle. Within months of moving to the farm, my father-in-law, Tom, drove up to our farmhouse in his pickup saying, "Robert, I need your help with a newborn calf. Unless we do something, he will die." As we drove back to the farm from Seattle, he explained to me, "The mother's teats are too large and heavy on the ground for him to suckle on. Same thing happened to her calf last year but I only discovered the problem after he died. We're not letting that happen again." There we were in a pen, our feet deep in the spring mud, heaving, coaxing, and pushing the calf to feed. Even as my clothes and skin reeked of newborn calf, I marveled at what it meant to be a student in this unexpected new classroom of life.

My urban mindset was being freed from self-confining assumptions as I stepped onto the terrain of an open mindset about my interconnectedness to this calf and the rest of creation. The result was a visceral new reverence for the fluidity and seasons of my journey with the Universe and others.

What if your intuition is inviting you to an open mindset about your future? Teresa is an accomplished manager who has always delighted in challenging and creative work environments that expand her skill set and infuse her with energy. After three years of working for a not-for-profit organization specializing in global micro-finance, she paid attention to the intuition clamoring for her attention.

Teresa had been hired with the assurance that the organization wanted her because she is an entrepreneurial thinker. Instead, she discovered that the organization viewed new innovative ideas as rocking the boat. They preferred to keep doing things the same way over and over again, expecting that the best and highest outcome could still emerge from past practices that had not worked. She experienced an organization that paid little attention to the human cost of the confusion and impossible expectations set for the staff team.

She said, "One day I named what was going on. I felt resentful. I was always anxious about meeting my goals; I was working far too many hours, and I felt constantly sleep deprived and exhausted." In naming the reality, Teresa opened space to listen to her intuition. An open mindset began to emerge in which she imagined her life and work beyond the confining realities of the job she was in. She said, I'm grateful for all I've learned about micro-finance and proud of my accomplishments, but my creativity and spirit need to be unleashed in a new work environment. I've begun to listen to my inner voice without knowing where this will lead." A few months after she resigned, Teresa felt her stamina return, and she found herself making choices to be let go of the negative feelings she had developed for her previous employer. "I can choose to be imprisoned by holding on to those feelings and so diminish myself, or else I can forgive, renew, and be open to what good the Universe is inviting me to give my passion and work for."

The landscape of an open mindset freed Teresa to offer and use her skills in a way that is life-affirming to herself and others. She said, "The thin place discovered in meeting my fears taught me that the Holy yearns for my best good."

Your choice to live with an open mindset may emerge out of a particular circumstance or it may exist as a way of being that you intentionally cultivate. Either way, you are freed to reengage with yourself and be present to shine. The world and the Universe need you to be an active participant in shaping the invitation to others to become more fully alive.

Be aware! In your dance of becoming fully alive, your mindset can keep you off the dance floor or invite you to new movement on your journey. In the surprises of an open mindset, the thin places are given room to present themselves to you.

Reflect:

- What will you do to allow your life to become open to the thin places?

- How will you be present today to the disguises of the Holy found in you and those around you?

- What if you grounded your life in your belovedness? Whose life might be transformed as a result?

Spirited Practices

- Name how you are present to yourself and others and how this cultivates awareness about what is being revealed in your life. Notice how befriending fear shifts your experience of your journey.

- What Holy surprises of love have you experienced? How have they allowed you to see the Holy disguised in yourself and others today? Share your experiences with one trusted person.

- What choices will you make to facilitate an open mindset? How will it allow you to be surprised by love and discover the wisdom that exists within you? Offer thanks for what you have discovered.

Turn your face to the sun, and the
shadows fall behind you.
—Maori proverb

Pathway Six:
Hairpin Curves of Life

My colleague Garth walked into my office and said, "I've been asked to make a request of you." I'd just come from a packed cathedral where I had led a memorial service for the victims of an Alaska Airlines plane crash. It was one of a dizzying number of requests I responded to in my three months on the job as dean of the cathedral in Seattle. I was unprepared for the hairpin curve that Garth's request would throw at me.

"The roving homeless encampment known as Tent City would like you to invite them to set up camp on the grounds of the cathedral," he said, as we sat at a table in my office. "Surely not!" I said to myself. This was the last thing I wanted to do. I could feel my conflict avoidance anxiety rising as I said, "Garth, you know it's media warfare between Tent City and the City of Seattle. We'd be jumping right into that if I invited them here." He responded with, "Possibly. The city wants to shut them down and have them go away. But the homeless in the camp are working folks who can't afford to live in the city. Would you be willing to at least meet with some representatives of Tent City?" I could not imagine why I wouldn't.

"There's no way to even think of Tent City coming here," I said to a friend as I reflected on how my days were filled with responding to an institution rife with systemic issues. "Perhaps this is a veiled gift tossed your way," she offered. I thought of the advice that a retired bishop had given. "Leading a high-profile institution can be seductive. Be sure to find feed your passion by doing something outside of the obvious," he advised, and then said, "I used to visit prisoners once a month. No one knew I did it, but they always reminded me of life's realities."

Those words echoed in my mind as I met with representatives of Tent City. "I'm a divorced dad," said one person. "On what I earn, I have a choice to pay for rent or child support for my daughter. My daughter needs my support and so I live in a tent for now." As I listened to the stories, a movie played in my mind with scenes of me worrying about where I would live when I arrived in New York 20 years earlier. Mental snapshots of my bedroom, the dinner table, and family gatherings in the home of Hays and Linda in New York flashed through my mind. Gratitude flowed through me as I reflected on my experience of their hospitality.

As Garth and I debriefed on the meeting, I said, "I've worked with the homeless in New York for more than a decade. What if I invite Tent City to set up camp, and we do something imaginative to try to step out of thinking homelessness is okay in this affluent city?" Garth asked me, "What on earth are you suggesting?" I asked myself the very same question. I didn't have an answer, though I knew that the possibility of being transformed into something yet unknown to me was the last thing I wanted to deal with. I felt elation and alarm.

To my surprise, the word "guests" was the focus of my meditation the following morning. As I thought about the many people who had welcomed me to Seattle and my new position, the obvious presented itself in a new way. I called a friend to say, "Invitations don't have to be linear or sequential. An invitation to Tent City can be coupled with other invitations."

An idea was hatched in me. What if we invited leaders from a variety of sectors to gather and discuss how to make real a dream of ending homelessness in the city? What if among those guests, the homeless were represented? It seemed audacious to me. As the idea percolated, I imagined the voices of skeptics. I could feel fear and intuitive imagination colliding.

One hundred residents of Tent City arrived to set up camp in the parking lot of the cathedral, with its sweeping views of Seattle and the Olympic Mountains. That same week, a group of 30 people gathered to engage their hopes and best thinking to end homelessness. My own "surely not" was being transformed into a collective "surely yes" with this group.

On the Sunday after Tent City's arrival, the residents held an open house for members of the cathedral congregation. Walking among the rows of tents, a cathedral member was tapped on the shoulder. It was the nephew who had disappeared for years. "I put myself into rehab," he said, "and now I'm getting my life together. I'm in college and working part-time. I'm saving for an apartment rental down payment." As they embraced and hugged he continued, "I've been ashamed of how I've wasted so many years. I was going to wait to see if anyone in the family would talk to me, and now this surprise of seeing you at my home." One member of the cathedral described it as "a surprising moment of grace." Before long, the story spread like wild fire among the congregation.

When I moved to Seattle, I was sure that my active involvement in responding to homelessness had come to an end. I would eventually lead a countywide initiative to develop a plan for ending homelessness. The hairpin curve thrown at me was one in which guests, grace, hospitality, and intuitive imagination had begun to meet one another.

Hairpin curves are those events that throw your life off-balance by interrupting your routine, security, and path. They shake you up, point to unexpected invitations, and draw you into new experiences of being embraced by life and becoming more fully alive.

You can choose to brush hairpin curves off, taking pride in your apparent single-minded focus. Or you can welcome them as a teacher who has entered your life because you are on the cusp of expanding your consciousness about the Holy present in the transformative curves thrown your way.

These three stepping stones will be a companion to your choice to trust yourself and the Holy enough so that the invitation of the hairpin curves of your life are embraced, not avoided.

1. *Reimaging your fears—they reveal bliss and a new normal.*

2. *Embrace doubt—the extraordinary life-affirming gift of doubt.*

3. *Be awake to life—hold the questions in your hands as you love life.*

These stepping stones will ground your intuitive awareness of a hairpin curve. By saying yes to a curve, you will discover yourself treading softly on the magnificent dreams of the Holy given new birth in your life.

Stepping Stone One: Reimaging Your Fear

"Do not be afraid" is a constant reassurance offered by angels to humans in many holy texts. They understand that fear is a common reaction to transformative moments because you instinctively know that an old assumed way of living is resisting a new expanded way of being alive. Fear is not the only energy at work in the Universe—as you choose to go beyond fear you become free to experience expansive loving and being loved.

Domesticate Your Fears

Involvement with issues of homelessness was the furthest possibility from my thinking. However, even as love casts out fear, so my fears cast love out. It was the people and stories of those without a home—not the issue or injustice of homelessness—that transformed my experience of being fully alive. In the hairpin curve and the resulting invitations that I extended I was at once both host and guest with our common humanity serving as the gracious convener.

My initial resistance revealed the blinders and shadow side of my focused and disciplined approach to work challenges. An embezzlement of funds prior to my arrival had laid bare the issues of mistrust rife in the institution I had been elected to lead. In rebuilding trust, restoring fiscal health, strengthening the ownership among institutional stakeholders, and taking seriously the mandate to expand the institution's public role, it was tempting to keep the blinders on and ignore the more expansive vista of life presented by a hairpin curve.

The fears instilled in us as children, or those developed as coping tools, easily develop a confining energy that we come to accept as normal. As I wrestled the hairpin curve in my walking meditations, a surprising childhood memory surfaced. Because of my parents' concern over a possible encounter with a pedophile, I was repeatedly warned as a child to be on high alert when using a public restroom. Though their desire was to protect me from harm, the deeply instilled fear had contributed to my acutely task-oriented and focused way of life. I began to name other fears, including my fear of taking an unpopular position. Conflict anxiety brought on vivid, imagined responses to actions I considered taking.

When you name your fears, you begin to domesticate them. As you become aware of how the blinders of fear curtail your vision of life itself, they begin to lose their capacity to hold you back from the light of your own life. The fear-based construct and the shadowy vista that fear concocts begin to be transformed as you reconnect with the truth that you are made in the imagination and liberating love of the Holy. With mindfulness, you begin to approach the hairpin curves of life with an open heart and imagination.

Suzanne was profoundly offended by the derogatory jokes, innuendos, and comments about immigrants, gays, and people of color made by members of her family. She said, "I cringe with each comment. I love my family, but every time I stayed silent, I felt part of me shrivel up." Suzanne spoke of being tormented by her fear of speaking up. "I've been raised to be polite, and the shadow side of that is my avoidance of possibly offending someone."

Suzanne's fear bumped up against her belief that you discover truth about yourself in the wide circle of human diversity and differences. In acknowledging her fears, Suzanne offered, "With every demeaning comment, the world suddenly seems like a dimmer place, when in fact I know that we need one another to shine brightly, just as we are." Weeks later, Suzanne said that she had come to realize that her own integrity, spirituality, and life were at stake if she did not find a way to move beyond silence and the fear of offense.

As she worked through her initial anger at the predicament she faced, Suzanne offered intentions on her daily walking meditations and on a labyrinth for compassion, wisdom, and courage. As she did, an epiphany slowly emerged: *I have a voice to trust and that voice matters; it is the voice with which to tell stories.* At family gatherings, Suzanne would tell a story from her life in response to a diminishing or offensive comment. "I talked about being at the wedding of my lesbian friends, or the dilemmas of an immigrant family in my church as they adjusted to a new culture. I spoke about attending a protest against the deportation of undocumented families or why I took part in an inter-spiritual community outreach project working alongside Jews, Muslims, Buddhists, Sikhs, and Christians."

Although some in her family attempted to ridicule her, Suzanne noticed that when she told a story about another human being marginalized, the climate in the room usually changed. With increasing frequency, her stories invited conversation rather than the continuation of demeaning comments. With each telling, Suzanne noticed that her fear of offending someone lessened.

In befriending her fear, Suzanne said, "I can differ in a compassionate and clear way without being scared to death of how it might be received. Instead of life being sucked out of me by my silence, I've discovered a new freedom to shine a light on how we think about one another."

How do you respond to your fears when confronted by those whose words and actions diminish another human being? By domesticating the fears that stare at you in the hairpin curves of life, you can make a choice to see in them an invitation to live more fully into your life's purpose. Beyond the personal fires of life, you will begin to shine ever more brightly with the radiance of your magnificence.

By domesticating your fears, you are able to consign them to the tool shed of unhelpful tools, as you become more present to intuitively knowing "in your bones" how to be embraced by the hairpin curve dancing your way. Similarly, you will discover that domesticating your fears will help you welcome your hairpin curve as a teacher who reorients your life to becoming more fully human.

Claiming Your New Normal

Fear is designed to keep you frozen in a state of routine listlessness—to keep you from yourself as much as others and the Holy. Instead of allowing this to be your experience of normal, your fears can be thawed, making way for the emergence of a new normalcy that is yours to claim.

The attention that a hairpin curve demands exposes the enclosure of normalcy in your life. My friend Dorothy is an accomplished composer, musician, lover of life, spouse, and friend. From an early age, Dorothy knew that music brought her alive and wanted to follow her heart's desire. Her father, a successful first-generation immigrant businessman, expressed his commitment to education for his children by paying for college. However, he did not view an education in music as normal. So Dorothy eventually put herself through college, graduating with a master's degree from the renowned Juilliard School in New York. "I knew I had to follow my passion," she said, "but I lived with this nagging sense that it was not quite normal. What power I gave to my father's view of what normal is!"

Awake enough to pursue the education that would allow her gifts to flourish, Dorothy's delight was tempered by the life-sapping energy of wondering if there was some truth in the voice of her father. Two decades later, Dorothy came to understand that the voices who try to hold us back are like demons roaming about in our lives. Her spiritual practices of naming negative energy allow her to greet the negative energy with a smile and know she is still free to create. Dorothy says, "It is now natural for me to be in love with the process of writing and look forward to seeing what will be produced."

Even as you are true to your heart's desire, it is easy to be haunted by fears of imperfection or afraid of what others will think. Claiming the new normal of life-giving and creative energy allows you to respond to the hair-pin curves of life, free of the disapproving, scolding presence of negative energy. You then begin to experience that the song of your own life is a gift of freedom to embrace the curves that invite you to a more expansive view of your journey and gifts.

Michael's wakeup call to claim his new normal was, he said, "Like an earthquake exposing a dangerous fault line in my life." His best friend had challenged him saying, "It is exhausting listening to you. Each time you speak, you complain about your life or the lives of others. You may have challenges, but surely there is something for which you are thankful?" Michael could have been self-defensive and chosen to ignore his friend. Instead he said, "The foundations of my life were suddenly exposed to me and they looked shaky. As I worked through that, I began to appreciate my friend's truth-telling as an invitation to self-reflection about my life and the spirit with which I approached each day."

Listening attentively to his own words, Michael was startled to hear the level of negativity that he generated each day. "My reflexive response to almost anything was to zero in on a real or imagined downside. It was not pretty but it was what I accepted as a normal way of living." Michael set out to create a new normal for his life. Every experience of each day was reflected on—a business meeting, coffee with a friend, time in his meditation group, the text messages he sent, walking his dog in the neighborhood, or dinner with his wife. Michael identified something in each experience that he was appreciative of and that he could offer thanks for.

During the course of several months, as he engaged in a daily meditation practice and in working with a coach, Michael noticed that the old negatives resurfaced like a drone attack whenever he was making significant shifts to the new normal of appreciative living. Michael discovered he could smile at their resurfacing and acknowledge their disruptive lure, while still choosing to live more fully into the normal that he was claiming for himself. Instead of being held hostage to the fears of returning to his previous way of being, he befriended them and diminished their power in his life.

Michael's transformative journey to a new way of being human was not made in isolation. "My coach was a companion along my journey," he said, "And I also began to discover in those around me affirmation and love that I had been oblivious to before. I noticed that I was part of a circle of life in which there was reciprocity of desire for the well-being of all." In listening to the wake-up call of his friend, Michael moved through and beyond his fears of a new normal. He discovered that the negativity that kept him from being fully alive could be replaced with a new way of experiencing his life and interconnection with others.

When you claim a new normal for how you to choose to live, you begin to discover the wisdom and delight that is revealed in others and in the Universe. The Holy within you is rebirthed, allowing you to move beyond fear and into an expectant, appreciative way of being. The world needs you to live in such a way; the Universe beckons you to shine in this way and your life is too sacred to turn back.

Discover Blessings in Disillusionment

Disillusionment is a cathartic bearer of blessings to be discovered in our lives. For many people, disillusionment leads to curving in on themselves in listlessness, seeking comfort in addictions such as food, shopping, or dependent relationships. Alternatively, your disillusionments will become a blessing when your mindfulness allows you to be awake to imagination that clears a more richly textured path ahead.

In your personal life, disillusionment may be experienced as you notice that your actions do not always align with your values and intentions. In relationships, disillusionment festers when love is breached or trust is broken. The disconnect between the values of a workplace and the practices engaged in can be disconcerting at best or rip apart your idealized image of where you work. In every experience of disillusionment, a veil is torn open to reveal that you are bruised by what you have discovered.

Bruising makes it tempting to choose cynicism or skepticism about others as you nurse the wound of something sacrosanct that has been torn. Often unwittingly, you distance yourself and become a fearful bystander to life when you nurse the bruise.

There is another response that births the reimagining of your fears and disillusionments. In the stripping away of a cherished belief or ideal, you are invited to a new awareness of your humanity as it is revealed in your inconsistencies. As you stop racing through life and begin to notice your own breath, your mindfulness allows you to offer whatever harshness you have toward yourself to the Universe, and in its place allow room for compassion, tenderness, and delight in yourself.

You begin to discover that the veil torn open by your disillusionments presents you with a choice. You can leave it in tatters or allow each tear to reveal an opening of compassion toward another. With each expression of compassion, the enclosing prison walls withholding you from engagement with others begin to crumble, reminding you that your imperfections invite you to discover oneness with yourself and others.

Bert felt helpless as he watched a few people do whatever they could to discredit their boss with charges of mismanagement laced with innuendo. And yet he was certain that the esteem that others felt toward his boss, together with admiration of his accomplishments, would expose the real agenda of those seeking to oust him, so he did not speak up. Bert believed that truth would prevail and the ugliness would end. It did not—and his boss was effectively ousted. Bert felt haunted by regret.

This hairpin curve upended and unsettled Bert with a gnawing sense of shame and regret for his naiveté. He lamented his passivity and felt he had betrayed his boss and the majority of those in the organization by not speaking up. It was a self-perception that he increasingly resented.

Instead of living in an enclosure of regret and shame, Bert chose to embark on a path of self-compassion. As he named his regrets, and recognized how he denied his voice and avoided conflict, a new awareness emerged. Bert saw how these choices prevented him from being more fully alive. Unless he could claim compassion as an active way of engaging with others, his desire for well-being, kindness, and justice would remain sidelined. In naming these qualities that he loved, Bert identified what needed to be cultivated and nurtured within. In his desire to make amends for his lack of engagement in the scheme to oust his boss, Bert discovered a new highly attuned, intuitive response to situations of malevolent intent. He has chosen to transform his disillusionments by embracing a proactive way of engaging, connecting, and responding to others. Bert says, "Without my profound disillusionment, I'm not sure I would have accepted the invitation to proactive compassion. It is a new way of being human for me that is life-giving."

As you practice such mindfulness, a great decluttering leads you to re-imagine your fears. The new normal for your life awakens you to the blessing of disillusionment. The hairpin curves no longer keep your life at bay. Instead, they offer an enlarged world vista on being fully human.

Stepping Stone Two: Embrace Doubt

Doubt is one of the grandest birthing experiences on your quest, signaling that you are on the verge of growth. Transformation is usually planted by the seeds of doubt that the hairpin curves of life reveal.

Doubt Births New Life

Doubt can be like a mosquito in a can of paint, spinning about with no apparent way through or out. The hairpin curves that interrupt your journey expose doubts about what you believe and qualities within you that you avoid surfacing. Instead of being stultified or racked by your doubts, they invite you to trust your risk, imagination, heart, and journey with the Holy. The promise of being born anew through your doubts is a sacred transformative gift on your journey.

In the hairpin curve presented to me, I questioned my ability to make a difference. I doubted my capacity to re-engage the issues of homelessness through mindful leadership. I also doubted whether the media attention lavished on my sexuality would make it difficult to be heard. It was tempting to reject the hairpin curve by seeking refuge in those doubts and to bury myself in the time constraints and the plethora of institutional issues I had been elected to address.

The first birthing of new life is when you awaken to the complexities that exist within you, for this is part of the enlightenment that opens your journey to transformative depth. The questions presented by a hairpin curve then become like angels going before you, leading you deeper into the mystery of your journey. You have choices to make at every turn.

You can choose to resist the questions. You can disengage from life and seek refuge in cynicism that walls you off from yourself. Or you can embrace doubt's opportunity and be courageous enough to love the disturbance that creates an unclear path to new birth. This choice is like prayer, where eloquence is never required. Instead, the practice of prayer allows you to cobble together words that unite you with the life-giving generosity of the Holy. More than cognitive brilliance, you bring your truest self into prayer as an offering, revealing with new clarity what you've given your heart to. So it is, as you lean into and embrace your doubts.

My doubts about responding to the hairpin curve were as real to me as yours are to you. They were also a smokescreen of detachment. In choosing to hold the questions in my hands, I was able to walk lightly with my doubts. In responding to the doubts, my own voice and imagination came alive and my compassion expanded as the hairpin curve birthed a fuller humanity in me.

Edith's family drummed into her the belief that as a child with polio, she could never expect her life to amount to anything. Their mantra was that she would have to accept a job offered to her out of pity. Edith refused to believe that this would be the only path open to her.

Abused and raped by her father as a young girl, Edith discovered a vocation and purpose in a career in social work. With a Master's degree, she relished securing the rights of those on the edges of society. On weekends, she would take car trips with friends, delighting in the freedom that her driving symbolized. The fallacies of the naysayers who had condemned her to an enclosed life were laid bare by the purpose and delight that Edith's life revealed.

Eighteen months after moving into a retirement community in Florida, Edith suffered a massive stroke. Her home and car were sold and she moved into a care facility. The face of confinement that was assured to her as a child appeared to have arrived. I wondered if she would have the will to live. A friend intuitively understood what the loss of mobility meant to Edith and arranged for a motorized wheelchair to be given to her.

Entering into the next season of her life, Edith became the unofficial counselor and chaplain to the residents and staff of the care center, roaming the hallways in her wheelchair and offering a listening ear and wisdom to the many who sought her out. When I attended her funeral several years later, the room in which it was held was overflowing with staff. Cooks, kitchen helpers, cleaners, nurses' aides, nurses, and doctors cried as they spoke of "Miss Edith," the confidante, friend, spirit guide, and mother whom they mourned. They spoke of her playful silliness and the dignity that she affirmed in each one.

Doubting the confined life that others proscribed for her, Edith refused to believe that she had no life purpose. She chose to not let the most debilitating of hairpin curves keep her from being fully alive, fully human. In her passion for parties and festive events, she invited others to experience this truth—the banquet table of life offered open seating to all.

Likewise, those who have instilled doubt within you about your brilliance and magnificence reflect their own disconnectedness from life and themselves. Their doubts are never really about you—but about their own fears. As you trust your intuitive passions for a life of purpose that the world needs from you, the volcanic ash of others' doubts will scatter.

✢ ✢ ✢ ✢ ✢ ✢ ✢ ✢ ✢ ✢ ✢ ✢ ✢ ✢ ✢ ✢ ✢

Your journey is measured by your willingness to be awakened to the doubts that your hairpin curves stir in you. New birth awaits you in those doubts.

Doubt Your Belief

Creed is often associated with a particular set of beliefs of an organized religion, but the word as it relates to the spiritual journey translates to mean what you "give your heart to." You live with a creed or an assumed set of beliefs about your life that are challenged by the hairpin curves thrown your way. Doubt is the clarifying, life-affirming gift that allows you to tilt your heart to experience what you believe with new eyes. If you were raised in the traditions of an organized religion you probably live with an ingrained assumption that doubt is a weakness signifying a lack of faith or trust in a particular belief system. Nothing could be further from the truth! Cradling the questions that doubt raises is a marker of the health and maturity of your spiritual quest, allowing you to live with the larger universal truths of the Holy growing inside of you.

My hairpin curve shined a radiant light on my assumed, self-enclosing beliefs about the priorities of the work that lay ahead of me. In doubting the belief that guided my work priorities, I entered a new mindfulness about how to be enlivened in my work. It felt like trying on wings. What I would give my heart to would become the positioning system for the compassion within—and an icon pointing to who I am.

The beliefs that layer your life with a shroud designed to keep part of you unawake and unaware are often so seamlessly woven into your experience that you continue to allow them power over your life. Guilt is incubated by many family systems and religious experiences living within you. Almost as a virus, this guilt keeps you off kilter and distant from the life-giving health that the Holy and the Universe hunger for you to embrace. It becomes a shadowy control mechanism lurking in your life, ever ready to gleefully rear its head whenever you make choices about a new way to be human and fully alive.

Constance became aware of guilt and gratitude competing to hold sway in her life. She discovered new insights into these emotions during two years of unemployment. Initially, she was consumed by guilt for not being able to financially contribute to her household in the way she had been accustomed, as well as a stupefying guilt about having free time. She said, "I didn't know if I was making choices in response to my guilt about family expectations to babysit a grandchild, or run errands for others, or take care of my mother-in-law." A clarifying question presented itself as she wondered where her guilt met the gratitude she felt for the support and love of those closest to her.

In her search for new spiritual grounding, Constance made new choices about her eating choices and exercise. She began to remind herself that gratitude always exists alongside guilt, and to name the guilt she felt aware of and to recognize how it tried to claim space in her life. The result is that Constance now makes daily choices to live from a grounding of gratitude. When she chose to run errands for others or care for family members, she said, "I do it out of gratitude, not guilt. My choices about gratitude shifted my search for work outside of the home."

Listening to Constance's story, Patsy said that she had fought the "guilt battle" for decades. She added, "Although I've intellectually rejected the tight hold that religious notions of guilt have had on my conscience and adult choices, I've still allowed myself to be sucked in by guilty feelings that have eroded my life decisions; they've kept me from myself and that's deprived others of my being fully alive." As Patsy spoke, she acknowledged that the religious mantra of guilt she absorbed as a young person often caused her to live with guilt and shame about events in her past. In Constance's story, Patsy discovered that making choices to live with gratitude was a path offering her new freedom and life.

How will you allow your hairpin curves to test, push, and re-examine the creed that you assume for your life? Doubting the unexamined belief that you have accepted as a given in your life is an invitation to live and love expansively. In daring to trust its invitation, you will discover that doubting your own personal creed may point you to more generous and grateful living.

❧ ❧ ❧ ❧ ❧ ❧ ❧ ❧ ❧ ❧ ❧ ❧ ❧ ❧ ❧ ❧ ❧

Surprised by Doubt

Life-giving surprises reveal themselves to you when you cultivate doubt as a treasured friend on your journey. The path of living with conviction requires little of you—it is a comfortable resting place where you reassure yourself that everything is settled. The infinite nature of doubt meets your awareness and curiosity about the sacred that lives within you, surprising you with each new unfolding of it.

My friend Marcie worked with an order of nuns in the inner city of Los Angeles. At daily mass, she struggled with saying the words of the Nicene Creed and eventually worked up the courage to talk to the mother superior about her turmoil. "I don't know that I can keep coming to Mass every day because I don't believe several things in the creed," she said. The Mother Superior smiled warmly at her and said the unexpected, "None of us do dear. It's all a mystery." Marcie was surprised by this response and relieved that the meditative nature of the service could continue to be a grounding practice for her without having to take on a rigid conviction that she was unable to.

Marcie's greater surprise was that she did not have to separate herself from the community she cherished who gathered each morning for the service. Being aware of her own doubts and then giving voice to them revealed to Marcie a community of people whose spirituality of love in action was more expansive than any assent to a creed or belief. Much to her own surprise, Marcie began to understand why this community saw the sacred in people without ever having to ask for adherence to a set of presumed convictions.

As I responded to my hairpin curve my doubts began to subside with each step that I took into the work around homelessness. Suspicion gave way to trust, and caricatures of one another were replaced by respect and compassion. I was awakened to the surprising reminder of previously held individual convictions transformed into an expansive oneness that sought the well-being of all.

Likewise, your doubts will invite you into being awake and expectant about the surprises of your journey. You will discover relationships that point beyond confining convictions to compassionate oneness. Where will the trusted companion of doubt lead you?

Stepping Stone Three: Be Awake to Life

Being awake to life is a choice you make each day. Too often, those around you appear to survive each day with an aching, dull boredom. Your journey to becoming fully human offers a different choice of deep engagement as you live awake with expectancy to life and its hairpin curves.

Programming Your Choices

Being awake to life in all its fullness is the navigation fuel for your day. Your sustained practice of mindfulness about what each day will reveal allows life and others to engage with you. Awake to the ecology of interdependence, your choices come alive in the mutual rhythm of life that connects you with the Universe. As you engage with life in this way, be alert to unexpected reminders that you are off-balance. I woke up one morning to a typical Seattle winter day of dreary grey skies and incessant rain that seemed to have settled in with depressing stamina. It was a highly stressful and bleak period in my life. Every word that came out of my mouth was a litany of what was wrong, hopeless, or impossible to deal with. My spouse, after listening to this for a while said, "So, are you going to remain stuck there or will you participate in creating some sunshine and light today?" The question was arresting—it felt like I'd been dunked in a bathtub filled with cold water and ice cubes.

I knew that the question was not about putting on a "happy face" or pleasant front for the day. It was a reminder that I needed to choose between remaining stuck in the mud of how I felt, or remember to be awake and mindful not just to the day, but to what my feelings revealed as I offered them to the Universe.

The litany of wrongs that I uttered that morning was a path pointing to loneliness and isolation—a path separating me from others and the Holy. Being awake to my litany of wrongs was a first step in choosing to reprogram my choices for the day. None of the real or imagined wrongs could reveal their lesson to me unless I was awake to them and the oneness invited by each new day.

When life has not turned out the way you expected, do the hairpin curves reveal blessings? I was a little perplexed when I first got to know Gwen because she referred to the blessings of her life in almost every conversation. I wondered if she was avoiding reality. For decades, she has cared for a daughter with mental health challenges, experienced the sudden death of her spouse who she still describes as the "love of her life," and has a grandchild in prison. Gwen taught me that the most difficult of hairpin curves point you beyond yourself in order to discover blessings within and around you.

Gwen says that she has been sustained and grounded by her belief that the Holy is revealed in the realities of life. She speaks of her spiritual "authenticity radar," guiding her to seek out people whom she calls real or gritty. Gwen says that the path of authentic living invites truth-telling about our lives. "The curves of our lives are viewed differently when we can be real about them; they're not some private burden or pity trip, but rather a way to be real. When that happens, I discover courage and wisdom with others. In the authenticity of it all, I am open to discover beauty and goodness," she says.

Instead of choosing to live as a victim or imprisoned by the hairpin curves of her life, Gwen has chosen to be present in the now. In her meditation time, she invites herself to be present to the blessings of the day and makes a practice of telling one trusted person each day about a blessing of that day. When I hear Gwen describe the blessing of a sunset, of a walk on the trail in her neighborhood, lunch with a friend, or her incarcerated granddaughter's joy at a visit from her, I understand that the blessings she describes are not an escape. They are as real and authentic as she and the hairpin curves of her life.

Likewise, the choices you program in your life determine whether your journey is one of authenticity or not, and whether delight and blessings are companions to whatever realities you confront. Your connections of meaning and purpose with others become part of the lens through which you choose to experience life on a new way to being human.

As you practice being mindfully awake, keep in mind that the power of the wrongs you feel, the fears you face, the anxieties that unsettle you, and the hopes you harbor are real. When you name them, you release them so that their power does not prevent you from being awake to the day and the invitation of a hairpin curve. You become an active programmer of your choice to be fully alive.

Embracing the Curves of Life

When you embrace the curves that life throws your way, you become awake to the sacred dreams spread under your feet and within you and others. When your consciousness is not aligned with being awake to the curves, you participate in resisting the dreams of the Holy awaiting your discovery. It is a choice that defines your journey to being fully alive.

I met Donald at a retreat I was leading. He leads a men's group in a primarily white-collar church that is focused on projects to improve the church's buildings. As we discussed his evolving awareness of the Holy discovered in the curves of life, Donald said, "My greatest awakening has been to pay attention to those around me. Karl, one of our men's group members, has been a surprising teacher to me. Judging by his clothes, we all assumed Karl was a construction worker, and we never intentionally made an effort to include him. That all changed one day when we discussed building or buying a new altar when Karl piped up, 'I can do that.'"

A week later, Karl returned with a mock-up of his design for the group to look at. Donald said, "My jaw dropped. It was magnificent! Karl made this passionate presentation about the design and building details for it. Here was this usually silent man speaking with passion for his work." Donald said, "When he gave us the timeline for completion, Karl expressed his thanks for being able to be useful and create something of beauty for a community."

Donald's assumptions and judgments about a person based on their appearance and lack of verbosity had thrown a hairpin curve in his life. Donald and Karl met several times over coffee to discuss the project, and through listening to the stories of one another's lives, began a friendship that neither man had imagined. Donald reflected that his own embarrassment at having sidelined Karl gave way to an intentionality about engaging with others that has shifted the way he listens and connects: "I feel like I'm more awake to embracing and noticing the surprises of life. Instead of trampling on Karl and his dreams, I need to tread lightly, because we need one another for allowing the dreams of the Holy to shine."

Likewise on your journey, the dreams of the Holy are illuminated when your consciousness shifts to embrace the curves of life and the surprises that they reveal bringing you and others alive. What will your embrace reveal to you and to others?

Love Being Awake

The annoying interruptions in your daily life challenge you to love being awake to the invitation they extend. Your mindful choice to see beyond the interruption or the annoyance you feel usually reveals a hairpin curve inviting you to remember your grounding.

I was on a tight schedule driving across the Cascade Mountains to Seattle when the traffic came to a grinding halt because the freeway had been closed for scheduled rock blasting. I was headed to a long-planned meeting and in spite of the ample time I had given for the drive, the road closure would mean getting to the appointment late, at best. I was annoyed and frustrated, and had no cell phone reception.

As I walked about talking to other stranded drivers, I realized that the closure would last for at least an hour or two. As I bemoaned what this meant for my schedule, I realized that I did not want frustration to be my companion for the wait ahead. I began to pay attention to my breath and took in the beauty of the mountains around me. Although I was familiar with the drive and the landscape, my breathing exercises allowed me to notice folds and outcrops of the mountains that I had not paid attention to before. Their confident, imposing beauty conveyed certainty about their place and presence in the universe.

As annoyance gave way to appreciation, I began to rethink the emphasis and goals of the meeting that still lay ahead. I was filled with new expectancy and delight about those I would be working with later in the day. The hairpin curve of an unexpected stoppage resulted in creative thinking that I would not otherwise have had the opportunity for that day.

Similarly, your love of being awake to your place and presence on the journey to becoming fully human will allow you to see beyond your immediate reactions to a hairpin curve and know that being present to the curve allows you to awaken to new awareness.

There is a story about the Buddha that illustrates this truth. Crowds surrounded him, demanding to know what he was. Some asked if he was a saint or a god. Finally, the Buddha said, "I am awake." The path to enlightenment allowed the Buddha to describe himself with such profound oneness between himself and the Universe.

I was bedeviled by a vexing problem with no apparent solution, and had spent a few days working on it, when one day Lucy, my Labrador became unusually insistent in her invitation to have me take her outside for a walk. As we played fetch and walked together, I realized that she had invited me to let go of clutching at the energy-consuming problem. It was impossible not to follow Lucy's lead, and smile and enter into the delight of the day. With a different rhythm of joy present in the day, I returned to my office to discover a simple, seamless solution to my problem.

I could choose to ignore the everyday invitations to be grounded in joy, but instead I keep learning that these holy surprises are a teacher. The result is that simple encounters—from a walk with Lucy to a child waving to me across the waiting room in a doctor's office, to lovers leaning into their conversation in a restaurant—become teachers, reconnecting me to the course of my life, passion, and heart.

It is easy to allow ordinary problems and frustrations to define your day. As much as you clutch at them, they clutch you in their grip. Be aware of how clutching detours your life, disconnecting you from being awake to it. Notice how ordinary moments beckon you to make way for being more fully alive. You will then discover that as you let go, the Holy is revealed in the now of simple joys and delights that reframe your capacity to be awake.

To love being awake is an expression of your intention and your consciousness about how you choose to be each day. The hairpin curves test and cajole you with their reminder that beyond the irritations or annoyances of the day, there is a path that beckons you. How will you choose to love being mindfully awake?

Reflect:

- What bliss and "new normal" will be revealed in you as you reimagine your fears?

- How will your life be transformed as you welcome doubt as a companion and teacher?

- What do you need to loosen the grip in your life and become more awake to life each day?

Spirited Practices

- Domesticate your fears by naming them. Now release them, along with your assumptions of what "normal" is, so that your conscious intention becomes reimagining your fears. Notice the blessings you begin to discover!

- What will you give your heart to? Make intentional choices, then share them with someone who understands your journey; ask them to help you inventory and celebrate each choice.

- Begin each day with mindful intention about how you will greet and be embraced by the day. Choose to be awake in the choice you make, and close each day noticing how you have loved being awake to life, the Holy, and yourself.

We cannot be present and run our story line
at the same time.
—Penia Chodron

Pathway Seven:
Holy Surprises

At 4:30 a.m., I bounded out of bed, filled with expectation for the day ahead. As I savored my first cup of coffee, I wondered if my notes for the breakfast conversation I was to host and moderate that morning with His Holiness the Dalai Lama and Archbishop Desmond Tutu were adequate. Feelings of honor and privilege surged hopefully amid stomach flutters as I answered the phone. A friend's voice reminded me, "Just remember that while they are iconic people, they know how to enjoy themselves—and they expect you to do the same!"

As I arrived at the breakfast location at the hotel, the lobby outside the banquet room was teeming with people waiting to be seated. One of those I greeted said, "This is the most memorable day of my life. I cannot wait to be in the same room with these two!" The lively chatter in the lobby reflected similar expectations. After testing the microphone, I took the elevator to Tutu's suite to participate in his morning devotion of celebrating the Eucharist.

Entering the room, I reflected on how many times throughout the decades I had joined Tutu for this daily spiritual grounding in his life. On another floor of the hotel, the Dalai Lama was coming to the end of his four hours of morning meditation practice. I wondered if their respective practices were what gave them courage and strength for the work they do each day. Or was there something else?

Tutu asked me to lead the Eucharist, which I gladly did. As six of us shared in the broken bread of communion, I looked at Tutu and thought, "Offering hope to what is broken comes from brokenness transforming you." As if reading my thoughts, with impish glee he said to me, "You'd better not be late for breakfast. You'd better go down. You don't want to keep your guests waiting!"

Four hundred and fifty engaged, expectant individuals from a wide variety of religious traditions chattered at tables in the breakfast room. As if on cue, the room became attentively silent as Tutu walked in, greeting people on his way to the stage. Someone leaned toward me and said, "You can feel his effervescent spirit traversing the room." With confidence I responded, "This will be a life-changing breakfast for many."

As Tutu and I began to discuss compassion, one of the side doors to the room opened. Tutu stopped in mid-sentence and said, "Here he is!" gesturing toward the Dalai Lama and beaming broadly at the sight of his good friend. On stage, they bowed to each other and hugged. You could feel the audience reciprocating their affection for one another. The discussion continued.

Then, at one point I noticed the Dalai Lama was moving his left elbow back and forth, poking Tutu in the ribs. I stopped in mid-sentence to watch. Finally Tutu said to the Dalai Lama, "What are you doing?" His Holiness continued poking Tutu as he said, "You've got fat! You've put on weight!" With that, they both collapsed into peals of laughter. I was mesmerized by this interaction, and the audience looked uncertain about how to respond. Then Tutu said, "You'd better behave yourself! Start acting like a holy man!" With that, the audience joined in the laughter. These two had gifted us with a holy surprise. We were delighting with delight.

Delight and playfulness open us to the Holy found in simple acts of delighting in life. No matter the weightiness of our workload or our feelings of helplessness, our engagement with life is changed when we cultivate delight. Nurturing awareness, awe, and openness to the magnificence surrounding us in the ordinariness of everyday life puts our demanding lives in a broader perspective. Delighting in delight is not only possible each day, it is your compass for being fully alive. Using the compass of delight along your journey will reveal a different truth about your relationship with the Holy.

⁕

The Holy delights in you. Even in the litter of your story, it is in the messiness of your life that delight invites you to be present to the surprising gladness of who you are. When you are aware that delight punctuates your life you experience yourself and others with a new gentle tenderness and appreciation. It is a reminder that life-shifting joy and gladness are part of your journey to becoming fully alive.

These three stepping stones are tools for your journey to the surprises of delighting in delight:

1. Expect delight—welcome it into each day.
2. Create with the Holy—journey on this landscape of your life.
3. Tend to your field of feasting—be nourished by it.

These stepping stones invite you to new revelation that you are one of the delights of the Holy. The many dimensions of your story, voice and journey invite you to be present to your own personal "life canvas" of delight.

Stepping Stone One: Expect Delight

When you practice cultivating expectancy in your spirit you shift the grounding of your journey. Expectancy is quite different than living with wishful thinking. Expectancy is about how you choose to receive and live life in the now. It becomes a landscape on which you are aware and open to the surprises revealed because the Holy adores and honors you. Delight reveals itself in you and others. The world needs your delight as much as you do.

Greet Your Teacher

When the palms of your hands are open in meditation or prayer you begin to live without clutching onto life as you know it or want it to be. Your eyes and spirit become open to the teaching of surprising experiences and people. Your choices will either keep the teacher at bay or allow you to enter into wisdom discovered in the extraordinarily ordinary moments along your journey.

Luis stood on the vast stone platform in front of a large church where he was baptized with his father and godparents, surrounded by other families whose infant children were also to be baptized that day. The usually reserved 3-year-old Luis looked uncomfortable at first, not used to being the focus of attention in front of a sizeable crowd. After several minutes, he began to survey the 70-foot-long platform. Then, in front of hundreds of people, Luis started doing cartwheels back and forth across the platform.

His father looked startled and unprepared for what was happening. Luis brought the service to a complete stop with the unassuming self-confidence of his surprising cartwheels. Some in the room looked disapproving as if they were the gatekeepers of appropriate behavior. A few looked glum or uncertain about how to react to something they had never experienced in such a setting. Most people could not take their eyes off Luis as this shy child seemed unable to contain the joy, expectancy, and delight of the moment.

Within seconds, most people were beaming, and then a collective laughter of deep pleasure filled the room. It was not the embarrassed laughter of those unsure of how to respond. Instead, it came from some place deep within. In that moment, laughter became the language by which adults could express their yearning for experiencing delight that is as expansive, fluid, and joyful as Luis's cartwheels.

A familiar service for those present that day was transformed from a formulaic expression of religion into an expansive glimpse of the invitation to be fully alive. Some discussed why this 3 year old acted so intuitively. Others were able to greet the teacher who had unexpectedly appeared to them in Luis.

It is impossible to hold on or clutch to life when you are doing cartwheels. What you are clutching on to owns you; your choice is to let go and enter into what the detour reveals about life.

For instance, I can fume within the mounting frustration of trying to extricate a check from an inattentive waiter, or I can open my eyes and heart to those around me in the restaurant. Seeing two lovers holding hands and leaning into their conversation or noticing a little child shyly waving at me from a neighboring table, invites me out of my frustration and into the delight I glimpse in these encounters.

When Lucy, my Labrador, insistently invites me to go outside with her, I can choose to stay caught up in a vexing problem, or I can welcome her as an unexpected teacher. Her abundant pleasure in fetching a ball or taking a walk is an invitation to stop clutching at the problem consuming my energy. It is impossible not to smile and enter into the delight of the day knowing that a different joy will emerge in the solution to the problem.

In moments such as these, I am reminded to be regrounded in awareness that my teacher, like yours, appears in the ordinary moments of everyday living. Life-changing transformative moments shift the core course of your life, but each day's delight invites you to be true to the course of your heart. How you welcome these teachers charts the course of your life.

If Only...

Life invites you to live more fully in the present. Yet each time you say, "If only..." you draw a boundary around your life, and enclose yourself from the yearnings of your heart. With each utterance of those words, you distance yourself from the expectation and experience of delight. It becomes a way of living in a shroud of regret.

Each time I am in a restaurant with James, he instinctively follows the same script. After ordering his meal, he turns to look at the food being delivered to neighboring tables and says, "I should have ordered that." As we engage in conversation, his eyes are always focused on the plates in front of each person around the table. Without fail, he compares his meal to what the rest of our group has ordered and says, "I could have ordered that." It is a metaphor for how James lives his life.

James is an excellent social worker who is passionate about his work. The emerging truths of his life involve discovering and trusting his own voice and celebrating it. But he says, "You ask a social worker like me to help and I'm right there; I'm good at it. But I'm not as good at respecting myself or allowing joy and delight to be real for me. I want those things for others." His self-image of unworthiness is compounded by the aching human needs of others that he responds to each day in his work.

The barriers to living in the present are represented in James's language of regret—"If only...could have...should have." Awake to this pattern, James now practices new daily choices that begin with naming his awareness of living behind a fence when he uses such language. His day includes short meditation moments using the phrase "Possible." His choice is to be open to the journey of delight discovered in the present.

There is a stark contrast between James and my friend Dwight. In restaurants, he frequently puts the menu down and says to the waiter, "Why don't you surprise me with what you think is the best item on the menu." I've never heard him express disappointment about the meal that is delivered to the table. Dwight's "surprise me" is a metaphor for his life and the choice he makes to be open to the delight and surprises of the present.

On your journey to becoming fully alive, your past shapes the image and narrative that you tell about yourself, creating a course for the journey ahead. Only you can change the direction of your journey. Your well-being and delight is essential to the world and yourself. Becoming free of your "If onlys" changes the landscape of your life, allowing you to replace a confining life of regret with a full life of delight in the present.

Claim Your Script

You are the author of the script that is your life. When you allow others—perhaps family members, a career, or religion—to define the script of your life, you live in a shell. Your face and name are presented to the world, but absent of the fully alive you. Your life depends on you claiming your script.

I was once defined by the script that said as a gay man, I could not live without fear of rejection and even retribution. I participated in the narrative of that confining script by not allowing the fullness of my humanity to be revealed. An air of familiar normalcy settled in to my being a conspirator in that script.

In my work and in the relationships with many of those I worked with, I lived in the shadowy space of fearing the loss of my job if I was fully authentic. A persistent nagging doubt questioned my well-being and that of others. I was not being transparently authentic. Was I willing to love myself enough to trust in the grace of life and the generosity of the Universe?

In my most significant friendships, I was true to that part of my script. Out of love and protectiveness, those friends unwittingly became co-conspirators in not revealing the real Robert they knew and loved. Yes, I lived with delight about many things, but my half-script kept me from knowing the delight of finding a new way to be human. Like you, my journey was marked by a series of tentative and then more assured steps into the light of authenticity. Like you, I did not have to make that journey alone. Those who loved me for my existence joined the guides and teachers who encouraged my next steps to become fully alive. They did not write my script for me because only I could do that. Instead, they helped me to courageously love as I claimed my script.

❖ ❖ ❖ ❖ ❖ ❖ ❖ ❖ ❖ ❖ ❖ ❖ ❖ ❖ ❖ ❖ ❖

I discovered that a half-script is a gatekeeper to life. No job or friendship is worth the cost of being kept from delighting in yourself and the landscape of delight that opens up before you. Harriett spoke about a transformative moment of epiphany in her life. For more than five decades this accomplished director, teacher, and producer had a recurring dream. "In the many variants of the dream, I would be on a stage directing or getting ready to give a lecture. I would be headed to a podium carrying a folder with my script in it. I would open the folder and discover that it was empty. I would wake up filled with fear and panic," she said.

As Harriett unexpectedly found herself working on the lenses with which she approached life, she was engaged by what it means to have an open heart and an open, imaginative voice. In announcing her transformative insight she said, "I've realized that I am my script. I do not need one to be in a folder. After decades of dreaming this dream, I can let it go." Harriett's relief, expectancy, and delight were palpable.

Your life is changed by authentically living into your script. When you choose to claim your script, you expand the half-script with which you have lived. As you embrace a new normal for being present to yourself, your lenses on life and the Holy bring a new freedom that includes an expansive capacity to delight in delight about the Universe and others as much as yourself. The world and those around you need this as much as you do.

Stepping Stone Two: Create With the Holy

You are a creator. Participating in the creative force and imagination of an ever-expanding Universe, your life is intricately bundled together in oneness with others and nature. A new way to be human is revealed in your creative intentions, actions, and engagement. As you create with the Holy, compassion affirms the oneness of all things.

Birthing New Life

Loving the world invites you to be a companion in birthing, nurturing, and protecting creation. The Jewish tradition calls this Tikkun Olam, or "a repairer of the world." With each small action, you birth a widening circle of compassion and so discover delight in the Universe.

On a sunrise walk along Barefoot Beach in Florida, I came across a group of volunteers putting stakes into the sand and placing tape between the posts to create a marked-off site. As I watched the quiet familiar rhythm with which they approached their work, I asked what they were doing. "We've discovered the footprints of a loggerhead turtle who came ashore to lay her eggs in the sand," one of them said, "The sign we will put up here tells people that this squared off portion of the beach is a nesting ground that cannot be disturbed."

I discovered that they were part of a larger group who volunteered their time to mark and protect such spots on the shoreline each morning so that human enjoyment of the beach would be respectful of the loggerhead's life cycles. Considering that only one of 1,000 every eggs laid results in a surviving baby turtle, my admiration for their work of oneness was deepened. Through their compassionate action, they were midwife companions to these creatures.

Every action that you take to be part of the cycle of birthing new life affirms the unity of all of creation. You become part of reminding yourself and others that our notions of independence are ephemeral in the face of the interdependence of all living things. New delight is birthed in you as you expand the circle of compassion for all.

Beyond Your Mask

Delight is always birthed through your willing participation in hope, and yet you can easily block your view of hope as you choose to hide behind masks that represent different spheres of your life. Your masks invite you to move out beyond your unconscious grappling with unresolved issues of your journey to embrace risk and experience delight.

Steve is an artist who accepted an unexpected invitation to be artist-in-residence at a juvenile detention center. Steve engaged inmates in creating self-portrait masks and chose barbed wire as one of his art materials. The warden was incredulous. "Are you kidding?" she asked. Steve responded, asking, "How can prison life be depicted without barbed wire?" As the warden observed the spark in the kids working with Steve, she gave him latitude with his materials. In addition to barbed wire, most of his young artists chose to include locks, keys, and chains in their portrait masks.

As he worked with these young people, Steve said, "These are not bad kids; these are people who have made bad choices." He knew that the life experience of each kid led to actions resulting in imprisonment. "I don't believe that a 17-year-old naturally thinks of robbing a convenience store," he said. Steve was determined that each mask be a unique, individual story.

To accomplish this, Steve shared with them the realities of what he had been dealing with in the preceding months—his own waves of grief about his father's suicide, the death of his best friend from AIDS, and the alcoholism of his partner. Stepping beyond the mask of his work and the inmate's perceptions of his mask built mutual respect between them. Soon the young artists were responding in like manner. The art of engaging with your mask "needs to be a fun thing to do," Steve told his artists.

The masks began to reflect the stories of each person; stories that few of them had articulated before. Soon Steve was working on similar masks projects with children infected with HIV, youth in a psychiatric facility, gay and lesbian adolescents who had come out and been rejected by their families, and terminally ill teenagers. The resulting Wall of Masks exhibit conveyed a hope revealed in the story told by each mask. These unknown and often feared young people invited human connection. A teacher said, "Bringing my students to see it has given me courage to not hide, but to address difficult questions like AIDS in my classroom."

Steve said that the young artists "Helped me to get up; they gave me a reason to be, to live, to hope." The recycled wood used for each mask became a metaphor for him of what happens when you move from behind the safety of your own masks into the risk of being authentic.

Likewise, your own authentic journey from behind the safety of your mask will invite you into a deeper shared human connection in which hope is revealed and new delight is revealed.

Explore Your New Landscape

Your journey invites you to move beyond the boundaries that you live with and instead think of your life as an unfolding landscape. As you test cohabiting with this truth, you discover a more spacious, permeable way of being human. Boundaries confine you while the landscape of your life is an expansive way to becoming fully human, fully alive.

Myra spoke about the liberation she felt in imagining her life as a landscape. She said, "For decades, I've kept rehearsing conversations with friends, family, and coworkers. The conversations are all from within my enclosed boundaries." Myra's life had been spent placating family and work tensions. She had come to believe that her life was defined by peace-making. "Except," she said, "there is no peace in most of these situations and certainly no peace for me. I'd accepted that constant low-level anxiety was normal, and I was always living on the edge, not knowing what firebomb might be thrown next."

As Myra journeyed beyond her old assumed boundaries onto the landscape of her life, she experienced a new freedom. She said, "Landscape transforms how I think about my life and the rehearsed conversations become quite different. If there's a rattlesnake within my boundaries I cannot escape it. If there's a rattlesnake on my landscape I can choose to take a different route."

In her new practice of Tai Chi, Myra was drawn to reach for new light in her life discovered in reaching up to the sky and down through the earth to the ocean and across horizons. It offered her a framework as a companion for exploring the landscape of life in which it is safe to explore a more permeable and connected way of living.

Your fears of exploring the landscape of your life may be centered in how those who are close to you will react to your exploration. Those fears can become an enclosing boundary keeping you from the very quest that your life depends on. Your life and theirs will remain in relationship gridlock unless you are willing to risk a way of being more fully alive together on a more spacious and open landscape.

Julian's exploration of his life as an open landscape collided with previously unexamined dynamics in his relationship with his adult children. He said, "I was certain I'd be tired of myself by now, but I am changing even in my seventies, and I don't think they want to know that." He believed that his children had a fixed image of him as a father. Julian was fearful of telling them about the changes in him that his journey revealed. "How will they respond? Are they able to shift their landscape of me or do they need to hold onto a static view of me?" he asked.

He acknowledged that he didn't want to be locked in to how he thinks about them. "I know that they are growing and changing, and I do not want to enclose them in a time warp," he said. Julian was yearning to know and engage with his adult children on a new open landscape—one that filled him with trepidation about their willingness to do so along with his fears of rupturing their relationship.

With small steps, Julian began to venture beyond the fixed time warp that he most feared that they would all continue to live within if he did not risk his heart. Through story and being actively present to his children their relationships have become fuller and more authentic than Julian had ever hoped for. Fear has given way to an expanded respect, love, and honor of one another.

As you explore the open landscape of your life, you can choose to be actively willing to go where your risk leads you. Some people will reveal their inability or unwillingness to be part of your open landscape while others will meet your risk and join you. As you trust your intuition you will delight in how your own willingness to be more fully human offers an invitation to others to be more fully alive with you.

Stepping Stone Three: Tend Your Field of Feasting

When you think of your life as a field of feasting, your way of being becomes mindfully open to the abundance that already exists in your life.

Instead of being captive to notions of scarcity you become awake to encounters with others that you receive as a feast. It is in those experiences of feasting that you are surprised by delight.

Explore Your Field

In your personal life, as much as in the culture around us, it is easy to be caught in the trap of casting blame, demonizing, and judging others. It diminishes the life of all, and you become a dour participant in shrouding the magnificence of yourself and others. Instead, it is possible to explore your place on the open field onto which your life and the Universe invite you. With expectancy you discover that the field is a place of unexpected life-giving encounters.

A parable in two parts tells the story of a missionary who goes to visit a distant village for the first time. Along the way, some of the villagers meet him and tell him that there is a monster in the field. Going to the field, the villagers hold back and watch him walk on it from a distance. The missionary discovers that the villagers are frightened of a giant watermelon. So he slices the watermelon into pieces and eats some of it. The villagers, terrified that he might do the same to them, kill the missionary.

In the second scenario, a missionary is headed toward a village when he is met by villagers who are frightened and tell him there is a monster in a field. So the missionary and the villagers run together to a safe place overlooking the field where they sit in the shade and discuss their fears. Finally they all go onto the field where they discover the sweetness of the watermelon together.

Discovering the sweetness of life is like the rest of your journey: it is always most vibrantly alive in the context of others. The playful, creating impulse of the Holy is discovered in the lives of those around you as much as it is revealed in the global human family.

My own consciousness of living on a field of feasting allows me to be present to the everyday opportunities I am presented with and to be present to others who invite me to share in the feasting of their field. It is an openhearted way of living in the present and being open to unexpected delight.

I traveled to the landlocked mountainous kingdom of Lesotho to spend a week of reflective time in meditation with a small monastic group of men who had established a remote community in a place called Masite. It was 1977, and I was searching for spiritual practices to ground me in my opposition to apartheid in South Africa. I had a nagging fear that the admirable but righteous anger of many activists could easily consume the delight, compassion, and love that had invited so many of us to work for dignity and justice for all. Intuitively, I knew that the displacing of delight is an amber alert that our oneness with the Universe is out of balance.

The solitude of the community was accompanied by an abiding gratitude for the simplest joys of each day. One of the members had been exiled from South Africa for speaking out against the massacre of school children in Soweto the previous year, and yet the weightiness of this cause was matched by a playful spirit of encountering others.

I was discovering that daily practices of meditation, together with a spirit of being awake and aware to life, are also what ground us in openness to delight. Right on cue, as I articulated this truth to myself, I heard joyful singing wafting through the air from the neighboring monastic community of women. In the laughter that followed, I realized that Desmond Tutu was next door leading a service for that community.

On my last night in Masite, the monks threw a feast to give thanks for having a guest among them. Surely it was I who should be giving thanks for the gift of the truths revealed by their hospitality? One of the chickens that they relied on for the eggs they ate was prepared for dinner, and a bottle of wine that had been saved for a special occasion was produced. As we shared stories over dinner, they thanked me for bringing news of the outside world and for reminding them that the Holy is revealed in every guest, because few guests ever traveled to their remote location. On my way home the following day, I marveled that my expectation of reflective time had been transformed by entering onto an unexpected field of learning and joy.

Likewise, you will discover that your openhearted, aware living prepares you for daily exploration of the field of your life on which delight is discovered and renewed by being present to others and the Universe.

Be Open to Feasting

You do not live your journey in the abstract. Your journey is made in the context of others. Food and beverages, from the most simple to the lavish, provide the construct for a feast. It is those who gather who provide the context in which you discover the love, playfulness, tenderness, companionship, and creativity of the Holy present in one another. Your choice to embrace the rhythm of feasting in your life shapes your experience of being fully human.

Feasting does not permit abstraction. Instead, it reminds you that your perspectives will be shifted by the grittiness of the human journey revealed in the stories of those who share your feast. Your perceptions of them are peeled back, inviting reciprocal authenticity. In the shared loves and losses of life, your willingness to be authentic becomes a conduit for delight.

A few days after my father had surgery, my spouse, Jerry, and I were entertaining friends for dinner. We had sat down for the meal when the phone rang. Jerry stepped out of the dining room to answer the call and in an instant without him having to say a word, I knew that it was the death call. My father was dead. Slowly the tears trickled down my cheeks before flowing in a torrent as a lifetime of memories of my dad flashed before me at dazzling speed.

Our friends offered to leave but I said, "Please stay; we need to eat; we need to be together." As our friends took charge of the kitchen and Jerry called close friends to tell them the news, I moved from being the host of our dinner party to a grateful guest. As we finished dinner, a few more friends arrived to offer embraces and love. We sat sipping tea and wine sharing stories of my dad and other deceased parents. The laughter that mingled with my tears became the balm in Gilead that the spiritual speaks of. Our impromptu feast was a moment of healing and courage for what lay ahead.

At the crack of dawn the next morning, I was using two phones to speak to different airlines about how to leave from Seattle that day to fly to Cape Town. In the light of the early morning, I saw two people walking up the front path to the house. Our friends Peggy and Juhani had baked muffins and scones for us and were delivering them with freshly squeezed juice and slices of fruit on a platter. "We thought you needed to eat," they said and added, "We're just going to hang out quietly in the living room or the yard to be on call for anything you need done." As much as the Holy invites us to play, dance, sing, and smile, the Holy is also present in the simple feast of sheltering embraces and nurture.

Feasts do not only take on the characteristics of sumptuous food and festive events. The food shared in life-changing unexpected moments is as much of a feast of sustaining love between friends as it is about the food enjoyed. Feasts that sustain, nurture, expand, and birth your relationships into new appreciation and depth are as meaningful as feasts involving abundantly laden tables.

To my surprise, a friend who lives halfway across the world invited me to our first conversation on Skype saying, "Come with your coffee and something fabulous to eat! We'll have a feast together!" I'd not imagined time on Skype as a feast! It is now our practice to bring to each Skype connection leftovers from a recently cooked meal and a story or observation about the meal for which the food was prepared. My Skype feast is a reminder that a virtual feast with friends and family can become one of many expressions of coming to feast.

Be prepared to feast each day of your life. Your mindful awareness about the myriad of opportunities to feast on the field of your life creates the possibility of unexpected invitations of profound human connection. Your life is never the same once you begin to be thankful for the feasts that beckon you.

Celebrate Time

Your celebration of time reveals your priorities about the relationships that mark your journey. You can make a choice to be capricious about time or you can intentionally choose time to be a trusted companion. Your appreciation of the ecology of time will allow you to spend time on the field of feasting on which delight punctuates and surrounds your quest.

Succumbing to the urgent but unimportant pressures of time can reel you in from the life that you are intended to live. When that happens, your life becomes a shell of what it might be. It is possible to instead be alive to the way in which time reveals choices for your journey. As you do this, you become at one with the sacred rhythm of your life, mindfully choosing to act on the passions of your heart and the relationships that bring you fully alive. You discover a new way to be human.

I do not get to see as much of my brother as I would like, because we each live on a different coast of the United States. I was elated by his four-day visit to our farm house in rural eastern Washington and set aside my work for his visit so that our time could be unhurried. It seemed like a slice of time to luxuriate in this creative, generous, and wonderful man.

In the uncluttered agenda-free time we enjoyed, I experienced new appreciation for who he is. In the spaciousness of time to be and to be present, we enjoyed the shared breath of spontaneity. On the third night of his visit, I was surprised to wake up before sunrise and find myself running through a mental list of all the work items I needed to attend to. In spite of my own choices about time, I felt ungrounded in this panic as the urgent tried to claim my attention and displace the important.

I could have succumbed to the legitimate urgent demands seeking to divert my attention and presence. Instead, I found myself naming the differences between the urgent and important, and offering thanks for uncluttered time. As I did this, gratitude replaced my anxiety, revealing new appreciation and love for someone I am thankful for. After his visit, I intentionally noticed how the rhythm of my life changes when time and nurturing relationships dance together.

In the days that followed, I thought of my friend Kermit who recently died from an embolism at a relatively young age. A passionate crusader for the rights of others, Kermit was famous for saying, "Live like you only have today." While he spoke from the heart about the causes he was involved with, he used time to do the same with those in his orbit. Kermit would pick up the phone or send an e-mail to tell you that he loved you or to simply encourage you in your work. There was immediacy to his communication, and a call from him was an unexpected treasure. A few weeks before his death, he called me to say, "I love you for who you are. I just wanted you to know that you are loved."

Kermit could have chosen to assume that people knew how much he loved and cared for them. Instead, he chose to express his delight in another person in the moment he experienced gratitude for them, no matter how busy or consuming his day was. In the afterglow of my brother's visit I was reminded that, like Kermit, we each make choices about where we fit into the ecology of time.

As you assess the way in which you use and enter into time your own humanity is enlivened by your expression of thankfulness for another person. Your spirit is expanded into oneness with others when you speak from a heart that gratefully expresses delight. You begin to live as though today is the only day that matters, and as a result, your own life becomes more fully human.

The deadlines of your work or those presented by family commitments are not usually possible to suspend. An employer or colleague will not necessarily share your views on the important versus the urgent. You have probably learned to integrate a life-giving way of holding these often competing tensions in balance. Your own daily spirit practices keep your lenses clear, so that you can be attentive to how your use of time does not sap you of life, but instead become a compass for your journey. The flourishing of your own humanity depends on it.

Julie had an unexpected wake-up call to these questions. A severe winter snowstorm brought with it road closures and warnings to stay home and not be on the roads for any reason. School closures meant that she and her daughter were housebound for several days. As she rescheduled meetings with clients, she was angry at herself for having left work at the office. She felt a mounting frustration at being stuck at home.

Her young daughter insisted that she go outside to play in the snow. Julie said, "I felt so conflicted. I was enjoying the spontaneity of the moment while feeling guilt and anxiety about not working!" Throwing snowballs with her daughter, Julie said to herself, "This is craziness! I need to enjoy this amazing moment!"

Instead of spending energy on placating her conflicted emotions, Julie chose to see an invitation to make a choice. She said, "I was creating an enclosure keeping myself from a moment of delight." Her daughter's glee revealed to her that fretting about a circumstance over which she had no control was keeping her from being present to the now.

Julie took on a daily practice of short meditation moments punctuating her day by mediating on a phrase such as "Be Present" or "Time." Each night, she would engage in an exercise of naming what she had been mindfully present to that day. She started to offer thanks for the experience of being present to unexpected moments. Julie noticed a shift in how she was becoming more fully alive and appreciative of time.

When the celebration of time is part of your grounding, you live your life open to the holy surprises of being present to the Universe and your life. Your engagement with others is no longer from behind an enclosure but on the field of feasting, where delight meets your willing participation in delighting in Creation and life. Your journey to a new way to be human unfolds with gratitude for the one life that you have now.

Reflect:

- What will be revealed to you about your life and that of others when you welcome delight each day?

- How will your life be transformed by creating with the Holy on the landscape of your life?

- What steps do you need to take to tend to your field of feasting?

Spirited Practices

‑   Name the ways you clutch at life or live with regret. Begin to visual-
    ize being free of them. Be intentional about being present to the
    now as you claim your script. Be willing to enter into delight each
    day and practice giving thanks for each experience of delight.

‑   Invite awareness of how you create and birth new life each day.
    Acknowledge the masks that keep you from being authentic and
    make intentional choices to willingly reveal yourself to trusted
    people. Imagine your life as an open landscape noting your daily
    steps beyond your boundaries and onto the beckoning landscape.

‑   Who will you feast with today and what unexpected feasting will
    the Universe present to you? Name and be grateful for those who
    feast with you. Mindfully pay attention to whether your life is con-
    sumed by the urgent or the important. Celebrate one example of
    your ecology of time that nourishes you.

The journey is the reward.
—Tao saying

Next Steps:
Becoming Fully Alive

Cape Town, October, 2011. The world is celebrating Desmond Tutu's 80th birthday. I am traveling from my home in the United States to join in the elaborate festivities in South Africa. More than 30 years have gone by since Tutu and I first met and joined together in working for a world in which the inclusion of all is celebrated.

Forty of us gathered in the side chapel of St. George's Cathedral, where Tutu led a simple service of Communion. Many of us had arrived several days ahead of the official celebration, and we were there to participate with him in the daily, life-centering, spiritual practice of Communion.

Midway through the early morning service, Tutu paused and said, "This is fantastic! So many friends are here from all over the world!" He began to introduce us to one another by telling a story of each person. "Jürgen is a medical student from Germany who has come to learn about reconciliation and work with kids with HIV.... Myra just came in from Sao Paulo where she is helping indigenous people tell and celebrate their stories.... Karen is wonderfully naughty and subversive! She teaches English in Myanmar, but uses the stories of the freedom struggle in South Africa and the work of truth and reconciliation to do so! Terry has just won a case against the South African government for corruption in arms deals, and he's been pushing and pushing at it for over 10 years, never failing to be convinced by the truth...." And so it went. Some of us had known each other for decades, and many were new to one another. Now we were all leaning in, listening to Tutu's gleeful vignette about each person as if meeting our cousins for the first time.

As we gathered in a semi-circle, laughter ringing against the stone walls of the chapel, my mind drifted back. I remembered the smell of teargas, decades earlier, wafting through the air as protesters fleeing police dogs sought refuge in this sacred place. In 1989, it was from this cathedral in which Tutu unexpectedly called for a march in the streets of Cape Town to say no more to government violence. I looked around the chapel, marveling at how this holy place had served as an incubator of life, courage, and hope for so many. We had come so far, risked so much. Our freedom was hard-won, at a significant cost.

In the same way, the journey to a new way to be human involves mindful choices that must be taken seriously. Your choices and mine matter. By the same token, the seriousness of their implications are revealed in how lightly we are able to walk with ourselves and others on the field of life. The freedom to nurture, cultivate, and choose is a gift that begins with you.

Freedom from something is always about freedom to do or to be. So—what will you do? Who will you be? Your daily choices can lead to living a conditional life or they can birth the emerging truth of your new way of being. There is nothing conditional about you and your life. Yes, you are still learning, evolving, and being birthed in new ways of becoming fully alive. And you are unconditionally invited to a new way of being human, marked by unconditional love and compassion.

✤ ✤ ✤ ✤ ✤ ✤ ✤ ✤ ✤ ✤ ✤ ✤ ✤ ✤ ✤ ✤ ✤

At each new step to becoming fully human, you have the opportunity to become more awake to the invitation of the Universe and the Holy. Ready yourself. Keep in mind that often the life events that seem the most disruptive can invite the greatest awakening. In fact, each disruptive or dislocating experience can become a path of emergence. Choose the emergence, and take with you some wisdom to keep in mind along the way.

The journey to being a new human is never to be taken for granted. It invites you to become awake and to stay aware.

In 1990 while living in exile from South Africa, my friend and colleague Michael Lapsley was sent a letter bomb by the apartheid government. Opening the parcel, he saw two religious magazines. Between the two magazines a bomb was hidden. Michael lost both hands and the sight of one eye in the explosion.

After years of working with victims of trauma, Michael participates in creating a Universe of reconciling compassion. He now leads the Institute for the Healing of Memories as a healer who teaches and enables others to be healers of painful memories.

Most of us hope never to share an experience like Michael's, and yet if you step back and withdraw from your emergent transformative experiences, your life will become listless and stultified as you clutch to the past and ignore the present.

Along my journey, I keep rediscovering the holy recipe for living an aware, awake, and mindful life. By indulging in moments of playfulness, mischievousness, and delight, I disarm and reimagine preconceived ideas. I dislodge distrust, and I uproot suspicion and old hatreds. The Universe and the Holy are not a sinkhole of despair. Neither are we intended to be. As you choose humor and joy, you create sacred space for meeting one another in a universal desire for happiness.

The journey to being a new human is never passive. It invites your active engagement.

As you actively embrace your passages of emergence, you intentionally engage in the new way to be human and discover new wisdom and truth for your journey. With each step forward into a path of emergence, your courage will expand the chambers of your heart and allow your spiritual positioning system to recalibrate and point you in new directions. With each recalibrated direction, your story intersects with the stories of those you have met in this book. As the seven pathways are internalized within each new insight and each new transformative, emergent choice in your life, they will evolve into an intentional way of life.

My friend Judy was at work at a refugee camp in a war zone when a helicopter drop of emergency food supplies went wrong, falling on her, and resulted in the amputation of one of her legs. And yet here, at one of the birthday events in South Africa, I was captivated by a group of 8 years olds who encircled my friend Judy in her wheelchair, dancing to the rhythm of the music with the radiance of joy beaming from her as she followed the lead of her young dancing partners. Nothing seems to stop Judy from actively engaging in being fully alive with others.

The journey to being a new human is never silent. It invites you to be a proactive, compassionate voice for the well-being of every person.

Your life and the future of the world are at stake. Because all are intertwined, no compassionate step along the way is ever wasted. Through your proactive engagement with others, you can do far more than you could ever accomplish alone. Your voice, imagination, compassion, and love will find willing companions throughout the world in creating a happier world of well-being and justice.

The lackluster leadership, corruption, economic dislocation, and political paralysis that characterize much of the world are an invitation to exercise your voice on behalf of those who have been marginalized or silenced. In this global hairpin curve, your voice, intuition, and imagination join those of others in igniting a universal awakening.

As you embrace humanity, you choose to be proactive in saying no to the forces who seek to reject the emergence of a new way to be human. As you choose to set aside silence, the old ways of being human give way to an emerging and proactive compassionate path for the well-being and happiness of all.

⚘

The day of Tutu's actual birthday celebration finally arrived, ushering in an eclectic fusion of pomp and pageantry, tenderness and love, shared with an overflowing congregation. The music of the cathedral choir and Soweto Gospel Choir filled the air. An impromptu sermon from the current Archbishop of Cape Town followed, as well as an impassioned message by the cathedral preacher, who spoke with tears and fervor of the gentle generous love that he said Tutu always invited others to experience. As he concluded, Tutu rose, and embraced and kissed him.

Following the service, a few hundred of us boarded buses to travel to a vineyard nestled up against the curvaceous mountains of Stellenbosch where an afternoon party would last into the evening. As a conga line spontaneously formed, I looked around at those dancing and smiled at the sight of our human chain—a feminist theologian, various heroes of the anti-apartheid movement, a human rights attorney, a school nutritionist, LGBT activists, and HIV leaders—all offering life, breath, and rhythm to the dance. Our joy was palpable.

Buddhists, Muslims, Jews, Christians, and agnostics laughed and ate together. Animated conversations marked the party as young people who teach within the townships about the prevention of HIV talked with guests from organizations representing the Dalai Lama. A stranger said to me, "This is the oneness I want to choose to live with every day." As we danced, laughed, and engaged in conversation, communion was revealed within us and among us.

Next Steps

Your daily life presents you with endless invitations to reaffirm your need for others and to make intentional, inclusive oneness part of the fiber of your being—a gift you share with others. Being a new human is your invitation to convene, celebrate, and intentionally create community in which the magnificent luster of each individual shines brightly.

Find, create, and claim your space with a community or a circle of communities. They might include local groups or organizations, as well as those that are virtual and even global. In community and relationship with others who seek to become fully alive, your collective brilliance is a declaration of hope, inviting others to discover a new way of being human.

Choose your guides and companions for the journey wisely.

Discernment about the communities whose circles intertwine through your life is critical. Choose those that are healthy and life-affirming. Detach from those that are not. Identify and establish the touchstones of community—such as compassion, love, and justice—that are vital to a new way of being human for all.

Choose your guides and companions for the journey wisely. Beware of those who clutch at life or hold back. Engage, instead with those who exhibit fresh imagination, intuition, and compassion. Detach from those whose energy is life-draining. Choose instead those who freely allow the life-giving creative energy of the Universe to flow through them.

Remember that none of your brilliance is diminished by the brilliance of others. Refuse to isolate yourself, for when you see yourself as an isolated individual it is easy to become cynical or distrustful. Cynicism and distrust are the marks of the old way of being human and are cherished by some because they devalue human life through disengagement. Seek out those whose laughter, delight, and playfulness invites new possibilities.

Choose to expect accountability from those in leadership.

The night was cold as I joined a crowd of mostly young people holding vigil outside the South African parliament buildings. The South African government was refusing to issue a visa to His Holiness the Dalai Lama to attend Tutu's birthday party. Now even a birthday party for an octogenarian was fair game—a throwback to the old ways of being in which apartheid denied freedom of voice, expression, and association.

Tutu publicly responded in anger at the South African government, which some found startling. He was obviously disappointed that his good friend was denied the opportunity to give a lecture on compassion and peace in his honor, and that the opportunity for old friends to play together was being refused. More than that, however, his anger was a healthy reminder that to guarantee the possibility of freedom we must choose to join together with others and expect accountability from those in leadership.

Our young people took this reminder to heart. Here we were, standing outside the parliament in vigil. This filled me with hope, as I reflected on how far we had come.

The South Africa I was returning to in 2011 offers constitutional guarantees of protection based on gender and sexual orientation. It reflects what is possible when the old system of denying the humanity of people based on race is replaced with a generously inclusive view of the value of every human being and the freedom for loving relationships of sustenance.

Choose to approach life with the eyes of love.

On the return home from the Tutu festivities my spouse and I flew via Buenos Aires, where he was to stay on for business. My connecting flight to the United States was grounded for several days because of volcanic ash blowing in the air from Chile. I found myself unexpectedly stuck in Argentina.

I surprised myself with how differently I responded to this situation than I would have in a previous season in my life. Instead of annoyed frustration about the implications for my work, I acknowledged that my work schedule would require serious adjusting. This freed me to choose to receive the gift in the unexpected. As focused and compulsive as I can be, even I have learned that it does not serve me or anyone else well to be trapped in the life-draining energy of frustrations over interruptions.

Choosing to be present, I delighted in the gift of time with my spouse, and experienced through his eyes a city that he knows well and one that I had never spent time in before. What I initially perceived as an interruption became a delightful gift of shared experiences and time together.

When you approach life with the eyes of love your vision is changed.

❖

What will you choose? How will you receive love each day? How will you share love by the way you choose to radiate life?

Transformative, life-giving change is only possible when you claim your place alongside others and shine light on the new way to be human. Err on the side of love, not right. Extend an invitation to share the journey—for the sake of the present, and in the interest of a future of well-being.

The blessing of the Universe is yours. As you share your blessing, and your journey continues to surprise, delight, and enliven you, the Universe will bless you with love and compassion. All are included in the intertwining circles of blessing, and the magnificence revealed will continue to surprise you.

Index

❖ ❖ ❖ ❖ ❖ ❖ ❖ ❖ ❖ ❖ ❖ ❖ ❖ ❖ ❖ ❖ ❖

Index

About the Author

Robert V. Taylor is a nationally known speaker, writer, and activist for social justice. A native of Cape Town, South Africa, Taylor was sent to the United States by his mentor, Archbishop Desmond Tutu, in 1980 to avoid imprisonment for his anti-apartheid activity. There, Taylor served in the Diocese of New York from 1983 to 1999, helping to build a community social-service center offering HIV/AIDS programs to veterans and people of color, in-home services for the elderly, day care for children of single-parent families, and a community music education initiative. Nineteen years after his arrival in the United States, he was elected to become dean of St. Mark's Episcopal Cathedral in Seattle, making him the first openly gay Episcopal dean in the United States.

One of the frequent themes of Taylor's public speaking and writing—overcoming enclosures—was born from an experience he had at 15 years of age, hospitalized for a failing spine. After two unsuccessful surgeries, Taylor was invited for prayer by the Anglican Archbishop of Cape Town, Bill Burnett. He was sent away with the words, "Your body will not enclose you again," and true to the Archbishop's words, it never did. Taylor told his story to an all-black congregation in Cape Town at age 16, and ever since then, he has devoted his life to helping others identify and break through their personal enclosures.

Today, Taylor is Chair of the Desmond Tutu Peace Foundation in New York, and also helped found the Committee to End Homelessness in King County, Washington. He is a graduate of Rhodes University, South Africa, and Union Theological Seminary, New York. He lives in Seattle and on a farm in rural eastern Washington.

An Invitation!

Join the community!

Share your insights, observations, and new human stories and experiences with us at *www.robertvtaylor.com*.